Level 2

4th Edition

Listening &
Notetaking
Skills

Without Audioscripts

Phyllis L. Lim and William Smalzer

With
Lynn Bonesteel
Christine Salica Seal

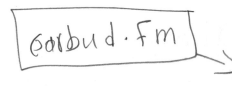

NATIONAL GEOGRAPHIC LEARNING | **HEINLE CENGAGE Learning**

Australia • Brazil • Japan • Korea • Mexico • Singapore • Spain • United Kingdom • United States

Listening and Notetaking Skills 2,
Fourth Edition
Without Audioscripts

Phyllis L. Lim and William Smalzer

Publisher: Sherrise Roehr

Executive Editor: Laura Le Dréan

Director of Global Marketing: Ian Martin

International Marketing Manager: Caitlin Thomas

Product Manager: Emily Stewart

Director, Content and Media Production:
Michael Burggren

Content Project Manager: Andrea Bobotas

Print Buyer: Mary Beth Hennebury

Cover Designers: Christopher Roy and
Michael Rosenquest

Cover Image: Paul Chesley/National Geographic
Image Collection

Compositor: Page Designs International

> For product information and technology assistance, contact us at
> **Cengage Learning Customer & Sales Support,**
> **1-800-354-9706**
>
> For permission to use material from this text or product,
> submit all requests online at **www.cengage.com/permissions**.
> Further permissions questions can be e-mailed to
> **permissionrequest@cengage.com**.

Student Book ISBN: 978-1-305-49343-8

National Geographic Learning
20 Channel Center Street
Boston, MA 02210
USA

Cengage Learning is a leading provider of customized learning solutions with office locations around the globe, including Singapore, the United Kingdom, Australia, Mexico, Brazil and Japan.

Cengage Learning products are represented in Canada by Nelson Education, Ltd.

Visit National Geographic Learning online at **ngl.cengage.com**.

Visit our corporate website at **www.cengage.com**.

Printed in the United States of America
Print Number: 01   Print Year: 2014

CONTENTS

SCOPE AND SEQUENCE

Notetaking Preparation	**Expansion**	**Unit Video**
• Number Notation	**Reading:** Crowding Our Planet	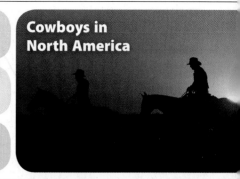**Cowboys in North America**
• Recording Dates • Names of Countries and Peoples	**Reading:** Climate Change Creating Millions of "Eco Refugees," UN Warns	
• Using Symbols and Abbreviations 1	**Reading:** Boomtowns: China's Instant Cities	
• Listening for Key Content Words	**Reading:** Female Empowerment in Brazil and its Effect on the Fertility Rate	**Through the Eyes of a Critic**
• Using Indentation to Organize Notes 1	**Reading:** The Geography of Religion	
• Using Symbols and Abbreviations 2	**Reading:** African Marriage Rituals	
• Transition Words and Phrases	**Reading:** Marseille's Melting Pot	**My Journey in the Muslim World**
• Using Indentation to Organize Notes 2	**Reading:** The Singapore Solution	
• Acronyms and Abbreviations 1	**Reading:** Can China Go Green?	
• Using Outline Form with Letters and Numbers	**Reading:** China's Sudden Prosperity Brings New Freedoms and Anxieties	**The Story of Hiram Bingham**
• Acronyms and Abbreviations 2	**Reading:** International Ranking of Systems of Higher Education	
• Reviewing Basic Notetaking Skills	**Reading:** Rising Numbers of Americans Study Abroad	
• Preparing for the Lecture by Reading	**Reading:** Bhutan's Enlightened Experiment	**Demon Fish**
• Pre-Lecture Reading and Key Words	**Reading:** The World According to Rome	
• Pre-Lecture Reading and Abbreviations and Symbols	**Reading:** Experimenting with the Jury System	

UNIT WALKTHROUGH

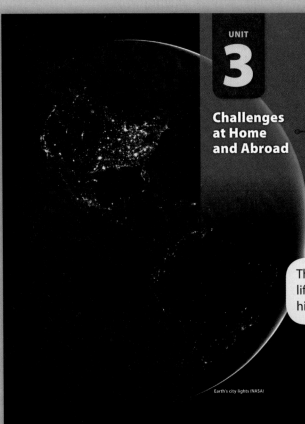

UNIT

3

Challenges at Home and Abroad

Earth's city lights (NASA)

The *Unit Theme* focuses on different aspects of life in the United States through lectures on history, politics, and the educational system.

Before Listening activities prepare students for success by activating background knowledge and providing the language and skills necessary for comprehension.

CHAPTER

9

The United States and the World

TOPIC PREVIEW

Discuss the following questions with a partner or your classmates.

1. Ten years from now, which country, or countries, do you think will be the most powerful in the world?

2. What kinds of responsibilities, if any, do powerful countries have to other countries?

3. Rank these three kinds of power in order from most to least important: (a) military, (b) economic, (c) political. Explain your reasons.

Coke bottle design contest held in Nanjing, China

BEFORE LISTENING

VOCABULARY PREVIEW

🔊 **A** Read through the sentences below, which are missing vocabulary from the lecture. As you read, try to imagine which words would fit in the blanks. Then listen to the sentences and write the missing words in the blanks.

1. Some experts are _____ that China will become the new global leader because of its size as well as its economic and military strength.

2. It seems very likely that the United States will remain very important globally, at least for the _____ future.

3. The United States can also help maintain financial _____ in the world because of the size of its economy.

4. I'm describing hard power—that is, the _____ or use of force.

5. This force can be economic, which would include _____ against trading with a country.

6. For better or for worse, the United States has taken on the role of keeping a certain _____ of power in many parts of the world.

7. The United States is also a member of NATO, an organization of mostly European nations _____ to keeping peace in the world.

8. ASEAN countries like Indonesia and Malaysia engage in massive trade with China and may at times feel a little _____ by China's size and power.

9. Soft power does not come from economic or military threat, but from how attractive or _____ a country's culture, political ideals, and policies are.

10. The United States is still a _____ to immigrants for both political and economic reasons.

11. My goal today was to give you a _____ for understanding some of what you learn in the media about the U.S. economic, military, and political influence in the world today.

B Check the spelling of the vocabulary words with your teacher. Discuss the meanings of these words and any other unfamiliar words in the sentences.

PREDICTIONS

Think about the questions in the Topic Preview on page 80 and the sentences you heard in the Vocabulary Preview. Write three questions that you think will be answered in the lecture. Share your questions with your classmates.

The *Notetaking Preparation* section presents a variety of effective notetaking techniques. Using content from the unit, students practice these techniques in authentic academic situations.

Notetaking Skills

Throughout the *Listening & Notetaking Skills* series, learners develop a wide variety of notetaking strategies necessary for academic success. Learners are taught the essential principles of notetaking and encouraged to personalize the strategies for maximum results.

Listening sections introduce the academic lecture. Learners listen to the lecture three times, focusing on a different listening and notetaking skill with each repetition.

NOTETAKING PREPARATION

Acronyms and Abbreviations 1

Acronyms are formed from the first letter of each word in a group or name. They are pronounced as words. For example, BRIC, which stands for Brazil, Russia, India, and China, is pronounced /brɪk/.

Abbreviations, like UN (United Nations), are different from acronyms and are pronounced letter by letter. Two common abbreviations usually used only in written language come from Latin: *e.g.*, used for "for example," and *i.e.*, used for "that is."

A Practice saying these acronyms and abbreviations with a partner.

1. NATO (North Atlantic Treaty Organization /ˈneɪ.t̬oʊ/)
2. ASEAN (Association of Southeast Asian Nations /əˈziː.ɑn/),
3. UNESCO (United Nations Educational, Social, and Cultural Organization /juːˈnes.koʊ/)
4. EU (European Union)

B Listen and complete the following sentences using acronyms and abbreviations.

1. Many countries have better economies, _____, _____.
2. _____ is an important arm of the _____.
3. France is a member of _____.
4. Some _____ countries are small, _____, Cambodia.
5. Some people think the _____ countries should become a federation, _____, have a political structure that is similar to the _____.

C Discourse Cues Number the following excerpts from the lecture from 1 to 5 in the order that you think you will probably hear them. Discuss with a partner or as a class the discourse cues that helped you figure out the order.

_____ First, let me give you some of the economic reasons Yetiv gives for why the United States will probably continue to be an important player globally.

_____ Now let's move on to the United States' use of what I'm describing today as hard power—that is, the threat or use of force.

_____ Professor Steve Yetiv of Old Dominion University in Virginia wrote three articles in which he gave a number of reasons why believes the United States will remain a global leader.

_____ Today I'd like to discuss the role of the United States in the world.

_____ Soft power does not come from economic or military threat, but from how attractive or persuasive a country's culture, political ideals, and policies are.

LISTENING

🔊 **FIRST LISTENING**
CD 3, TR 15

Listen to the lecture and take notes. Look at the lecturer's visual aids as you listen. These may help you understand parts of the lecture.

Introduction

The U.S. and the World
- Introduction
- The U.S. economy
- U.S. hard power
- U.S. soft power

Subtopic 1: _____

Economic Reasons
- Ability to help others in crisis
- Ability to maintain financial stability
- U.S. dollar = global currency

Subtopic 2: _____

Hard Power
- Middle East
- NATO
- ASEAN

Subtopic 3: _____

Soft Power
- Democracy
- Economic competitiveness
- Education

🔊 **SECOND LISTENING**
CD 3, TR 16

Listen to the lecture again and make your notes as complete as possible.

THIRD LISTENING

🔊 **A** You will hear part of the lecture again. Listen and complete the notes by adding
CD 3, TR 17   the information from the box.

ASEAN	econ	force	Mid	NATO	wrld	&

Hard Power = threat or use of _____
- _____
    sanctions
- mil
    US role = bal of power in
    - _____ East (free flow of oil)
    - Europe — _____ (organ of Eur ntns keep peace in wrld)
    - Asia — bal bet. ASEAN _____ China
        _____ incld e.g. Indonesia, Malaysia

B Compare your answers with a partner. Then compare the notes in **A** with the notes you took for this part of the lecture.

Unit Walkthrough vii

After Listening sections provide learners with opportunities to test their knowledge of the lecture and to discuss its content through pair and group activities.

The *Oral Summary* asks learners to use their notes to reconstruct the content of the lecture.

Through guided prompts, *Discussion* activities provide opportunities for learners to hone communicative and critical thinking skills.

An *Expansion* section in each chapter includes high-interest National Geographic articles that present information related to the unit theme.

AFTER LISTENING

ACCURACY CHECK

A Listen to the following questions, and write short answers. Use your notes. You will hear each question one time only.

1. _____
2. _____
3. _____
4. _____
5. _____
6. _____
7. _____
8. _____
9. _____
10. _____

B Check your answers with your teacher. If your score is less than 70 percent, you may need to listen to the lecture again and rewrite some of your notes.

ORAL SUMMARY

Use your notes to create an oral summary of the lecture with your partner. As you work together, add details to your notes that your partner included but you had missed.

DISCUSSION

Discuss the following questions with a classmate or in a small group.

1. Which of the four BRIC nations, besides China, is most likely to be the next superpower?
2. Would the world be a safer place if the United States were less powerful?
3. In what ways are economic sanctions preferable to military force?
4. What are the advantages of having more than one superpower in the world? What are the disadvantages?

EXPANSION

PRE-READING

The following Reading is about China's rapid economic growth. Before you read, answer the following questions. Share your answers with a classmate.

1. Look at the title of the article. What do you think "Go Green" means?
2. Scan the article for sentences that mention the United States. What comparisons does the writer make between the United States and China?

READING

Now read the article.

Can China Go Green?

Rizhao, in Shandong Province, is one of the hundreds of Chinese cities beginning to really grow. The road into town is eight-lanes wide, even though at the moment there's not much traffic. But the port is very busy. A big sign tells the residents to "build a civilized city and be a civilized citizen."

Rizhao is the kind of place that has scientists around the world deeply worried—China's rapid growth and new wealth are pushing carbon emissions higher and higher. It's the kind of growth that has led China to pass the United States to become the world's largest source of global warming gases.

And yet, after lunch at the Guangdian Hotel, the city's chief engineer, Yu Haibo, led me to the roof of the restaurant for another view. First we climbed over the hotel's solar-thermal system, a system that takes the sun's energy and turns it into all the hot water the kitchen and 102 rooms can possibly use. Then, from the edge of the roof, we looked at the view of the spreading skyline. On top of every single building a similar solar system could be seen. Solar is in at least 95 percent of all the buildings, Yu said proudly. "Some people say 99 percent, but I'm shy to say that."

Whatever the percentage, it's impressive—outside Honolulu, no city in the United States even comes close. China now leads the planet in energy produced by renewable solar and wind energy sources.

So, which is true? Is China the world's largest producer of global warming gases? Or is it the world's largest producer of renewable energy? The truth is, it's both.

Here's what we know: China is growing faster than any other big country has ever grown before, and that growth is opening real opportunities for environmental progress. Because it's putting up so many new buildings and power plants, the country can incorporate the latest technology more easily than countries with more mature economies. It's not just solar and wind energy. Some 25 Chinese cities are putting in subway systems or adding to existing ones. High-speed rail tracks are spreading in every direction. But all that growth takes lots of steel and cement, and as a result pours carbon into the air, which overwhelms the environmental progress. According to many energy experts, China's carbon emissions will continue to rise until at least 2030. This means that environmental progress in China will probably come too late to prevent more dramatic global warming, which could lead to environmental disasters such as the melting of the Himalayan glaciers and the rise of the seas.

It's a dark picture. Changing it in any real way will require change beyond China—most important, some kind of international agreement involving economies that use the most carbon—including of course the United States. At the moment China is taking steps that make sense for both the environment and its economy. "Why would they want to waste energy?" Deborah Seligsohn of the World Resources Institute asked, adding that "if the U.S. changed the game in a fundamental way—if it really committed to dramatic reductions—then China would look beyond its domestic interests and perhaps go much further." But for the moment, China's growth will continue, a roaring fire that throws off green sparks but burns with dangerous heat.

DISCUSSION

Discuss these questions with a classmate.

1. How is the focus of the lecture different from the focus of the article? Are there topics in the reading that are not mentioned in the lecture? Are there topics in the lecture that are not mentioned in the reading?
2. Do you think the author of the article would agree with the lecturer's view of the importance of the United States as a global power? Why or why not?
3. Do you think the lecturer would agree with the author of the article about the importance of China as a global power? Why or why not?

PURSUING THE TOPIC

Explore the topic of this chapter further by doing the following.

Watch a short YouTube video in which Professor Joseph Nye from Harvard's Kennedy School of Government speaks to Knoowii TV about the use of hard power, soft power, and smart power in international relations. Be prepared to discuss the ideas in the video with your classmates.

www.youtube.com/watch?v=cH9hn3_Q4qQ

In *Pursuing the Topic*, students are encouraged to go online or watch a movie to explore further the topic of the lecture.

Unit Video

Each unit ends with an authentic **National Geographic** video that is related to the unit theme. Most of the videos are in a lecture format, giving students a further opportunity to practice notetaking skills.

UNIT 3 VIDEO
My Journey in the Muslim World

TOPIC PREVIEW

Alexandra Avakian is a photojournalist. She was asked to take photographs of Muslims living in the United States. Answer the following questions with a partner.

1. What images or scenes would you expect to see in her photographs?
2. What different types of people would you expect to see in her photographs?
3. Do you think that Muslims in America have more or fewer difficulties than other immigrants living in the United States? Why or why not?

VOCABULARY PREVIEW

Ⓐ Read the definitions of these key words and phrases that you will hear during the video.

engaged in actively involved in or part of something
an expert a person having a lot of knowledge about a particular topic
post 9/11 after the September 11, 2001, attack on the United States
fled left an area quickly in order to escape danger
reflected shown on a surface such as a mirror; seen in a person's expression
mainstream average; usual for the typical people in a group
are converting to are changing from one belief system, such as a religion, to a new one
maximum-security prison a prison where the most dangerous criminals are kept
protective keeping someone or something safe from harm

Ⓑ Work with a partner and write in the blank the word from the box that completes the sentence.

artistic	civil war	pressure	security
Catholics	granddaughter	relatives	village

1. The _____ she was under was **reflected** in her face.
2. The man was not an **expert** photographer, but his photos were very _____.
3. The _____ were very **protective** of their young _____.
3. **Post 9/11**, there has been increased _____ at U.S. airports.
4. There are **mainstream** _____ who **are converting to** Islam.
5. The whole _____ was very **engaged in** preparations for the fair.
6. Some people **fled** during the _____; others were placed in a **maximum-security prison**.

🖵 FIRST VIEWING

Watch the video, and then compare your first impressions with a partner. Talk about what you remember, what surprised you, and what interested you.

🖵 SECOND VIEWING

Watch the video again. Listen for the missing words and write them in the blanks.

1. I hope to _____ a wider view of a group of people much misunderstood, especially _____ 9/11.
2. And these are Ryazan _____, and they're an alternative, Islamic alternative to Barbie.
3. And you know Muslim Americans, like all Americans, have fled civil war, dictatorship, _____ hardship.
4. These are Persian Americans, Iranian Americans, and they jump over _____ on their New Year to cast off the bad luck of the previous year, you know, for good luck in the _____ year.

Islamic Center, Dearborn, Michigan

Listening and Notetaking Skills Series Components

The Audio CDs provide all the lectures and listening activities contained in the Student Book.

The Video DVD contains five authentic **National Geographic** videos relating to the units in the book.

The Face of the People

CHAPTER 1

The Population

TOPIC PREVIEW

Answer the following questions with a partner or your classmates.

1. Do the people you see in the picture here match your idea of the kinds of people who live in the United States? In what ways?

2. Do you think there are more old people or more young people in the United States?

3. Would you guess that the U.S. population has increased or decreased since the census in 2010? Why?

Travelers arrive at Grand Central Terminal in New York.

VOCABULARY PREVIEW

CD 1, TR 1

A Read through the sentences below, which are missing vocabulary from the lecture. As you read, try to imagine which words would fit in the blanks. Then listen to the sentences and write the missing words in the blanks.

1. Most countries take a _____ every 10 years or so in order to count the people and to know where they are living.

2. A country with a growing population is a country that is becoming more _____.

3. A person's _____ is partly determined by skin color and type of hair as well as other physical characteristics.

4. The majority of the U.S. population is of European _____.

5. The _____ distribution of a country's population gives information about where the people are living.

6. Many different kinds of people _____ the total U.S. population. In other words, people of different races and ages _____ up the population.

7. The median age of the U.S. population, which is a _____ large one, has been getting _____ higher recently.

8. _____ areas are more _____ populated than rural areas. That is, they have more people per square mile.

9. I want to discuss the distribution of the U.S. population in terms of age and _____.

10. In fact, _____, women generally live longer than men worldwide.

11. A country whose _____ rate is higher than its death rate will have an _____ population.

12. On the average, women have a higher life _____ than men do.

B Check the spelling of the vocabulary words with your teacher. Discuss the meanings of these words and any other unfamiliar words in the sentences.

PREDICTIONS

Think about the questions in the Topic Preview on page 2 and the sentences you heard in the Vocabulary Preview. Write three questions that you think will be answered in the lecture. Share your questions with your classmates.

NOTETAKING PREPARATION

Number Notation

During a lecture, you will sometimes need to write down many numbers. They may be expressed as whole numbers, percentages, fractions, or ratios. Here are some ways to write them as numerals when you are taking notes.

Whole numbers:	thirty-seven million	37 mill. or 37M
	four hundred ninety-five thousand	495,000 or 495 thou or 495K
Fractions:	three-fourths, three-quarters	3/4
	two-thirds	2/3
	one and a half	1 1/2
Percentages:	thirteen point four percent	13.4%
	zero point nine percent	0.9%
Ratios:	two out of ten	2:10

🔊 **A** You will hear ten numbers. As you listen, write them in notetaking form in the spaces below.

CD 1, TR 2

1. _____ 6. _____

2. _____ 7. _____

3. _____ 8. _____

4. _____ 9. _____

5. _____ 10. _____

Discourse Cues   A discourse cue is a word, phrase, or sentence that a lecturer uses to help you follow the flow of ideas in a lecture. It often lets you know that a new subtopic or point is being introduced.

B Number the following excerpts from the lecture from 1 to 5 in the order that you think you will probably hear them. Discuss with a partner or as a class the discourse cues that helped you figure out the order.

_____ Another way of looking at the population is by geographical distribution.

_____ Today we're going to talk about population in the United States.

_____ First of all, let's take a look at the population by race and origin.

_____ Now, to finish up this section on geographical distribution, consider that about 83 percent of the people live in metropolitan areas,

_____ Before we finish today, I want to discuss the distribution of the U.S. population in terms of age and gender.

FIRST LISTENING

🔊
CD 1, TR 3

A Listen to the beginning of the lecture. Circle the set of notes below that best records the information you hear.

a.

> Pop of US
> 2010, 309M (27M more since 2000)
>   US 3rd most pop in wrld
>   most PRCh, 2nd India, 4 Indonesia, 5
>   Brazil, 6 Pakistan
> US pop — look at 3 ways
>   Race & origin — % wht/blk/etc; where fr
>   Geog. distrib — where live
>   Age & gender

b.

> US gov't census 2010
>   US pop = 309M — 27M more 2000
>   US 3rd most pop in wrld
>   1st China
>   2nd India
>   4th 5th 6th — Indonesia Brazil Pakistan
>   In notes — 1st pop by race and origin, 2nd
>   by geographical distribution, last by age and
>   gender

🔊
CD 1, TR 4

B Now listen to the whole lecture and take notes. Look at the lecturer's visual aids as you listen. These may help you understand parts of the lecture.

Subtopic 1: _Population by Race and Origin_

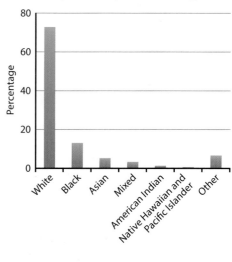

US Population by Race and Origin

Subtopic 2: _Population by Geographical Distribution_

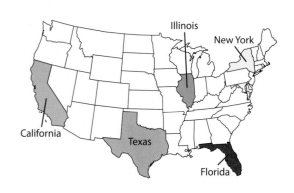

Chapter 1 · **The Population** 5

Subtopic 3: <u>Population by Age and Gender</u>

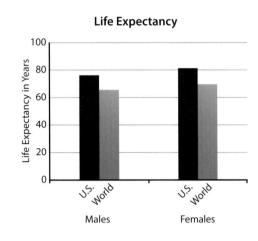

Life Expectancy

🔊
CD 1, TR 5

SECOND LISTENING

Listen to the lecture again and make your notes as complete as possible.

THIRD LISTENING

🔊
CD 1, TR 6

Ⓐ You will hear part of the lecture again. Listen and complete the notes by adding the information from the box.

| 19M– | 2:10 | pop | metro | TEX | W. |

5 most pop states:
   CA 37M+; _____ 25M+; NY 19M+; FL _____; ILL 13M
- 50%+ pop in S. & _____
   But E = more dense _____
- 83% in _____ areas (LA, NY, Chicago, Houston)
   < _____ in rural areas

Ⓑ Compare your answers with a partner. Then compare the notes in **A** with the notes you took for this part of the lecture.

ACCURACY CHECK

CD 1, TR 7

A Listen to the following questions, and write short answers. Use your notes. You will hear each question one time only.

1. _____
2. _____
3. _____
4. _____
5. _____
6. _____
7. _____
8. _____
9. _____
10. _____

B Check your answers with your teacher. If your score is less than 70 percent, you may need to listen to the lecture again and rewrite some of your notes.

ORAL SUMMARY

Use your notes to create an oral summary of the lecture with your partner. As you work together, add details to your notes that your partner included but you had missed.

DISCUSSION

Discuss the following questions with a classmate or in a small group.

1. What points in the lecture surprised you? Why?

2. In what ways do you think the U.S. population will change in the future?

3. What population problems do other countries you know about face, for example, in terms of origins, age, or number of males and females?

4. What population issues might become more important as the world moves toward a population of 8 billion people?

PRE-READING

The following Reading is about population trends. Before you read, answer the following questions. Share your answers with a classmate.

1. The lecture was about the U.S. population. Look at the title of the article. What population will it be about? How do you think the author sees that population changing?

2. In what ways do you think worldwide population trends might be similar to U.S. population trends? In what ways might they differ?

READING

Now read the article.

Crowding Our Planet

As of 2009, there were 6.8 billion people in the world. This is twice the number of the population in 1960, and four times as much as 100 years ago. As a result, more and more places on the globe are incredibly crowded. This is especially true of cities along the coasts, where more and more people are settling. Yet a full city today can mean an empty village or town across the country, or on the other side of the world. Our growth has taken place in surprising ways.

The human population continues to expand by more than 200,000 people every day. There are more than 1 billion teenagers in the world today who will soon be having children. As a result, we can expect the boom in births to continue for a long time. The UN estimates that the global population will reach 9.2 billion by the middle of this century. Even that enormous number may be too small, however, since it is based on the theory that family sizes will drop throughout developing regions—a theory that may not turn out to be true.

From the crowded streets of Lagos and Mumbai (Bombay), to the suburbs of the United States, to disappearing tropical forests

Rio de Janeiro, Brazil

around the world, the harmful effects of more people than the planet can comfortably support are obvious almost anywhere we look.

Not all countries grow the same, of course. Almost all of the expected population increase in the near future will come in developing countries. In the advanced economies in much of Europe, however, where rapid growth started with the industrial revolution two centuries ago, and in Korea, Japan, and elsewhere, national populations are stable or, in some cases, are even getting smaller. This brings challenges of its own, as newer generations struggle to care for and support their elders.

Humanity is also on the move as never before. More than 3 percent of the global population—more than 200 million people—live outside their country of birth. Many millions more have moved, or been moved, within their home borders.

Our numbers and our mobility, together with improved communication, all make Earth seem smaller, even as our impact on it grows larger every

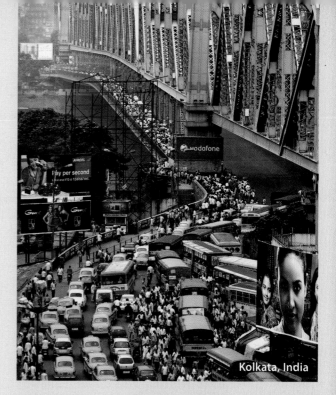

Kolkata, India

day. If we are to preserve the biological wealth of our planet and increase the well-being of its people, we must first understand how and why our own population is changing.

DISCUSSION

Discuss these questions with a classmate.

1. Based on what you know, which countries or regions mentioned in the article have populations that are most similar to the population of the United States? Which are the least similar?

2. Which of the U.S. population trends mentioned in the lecture are also true for the world population? Discuss race and origin, geographic distribution, and age and gender.

3. What problems related to population are mentioned in the article? Which of these problems apply to the United States?

PURSUING THE TOPIC

Explore the topic of this chapter further by doing the following.

Individually or with a partner, research population trends—racial composition, geographic distribution, age, and gender—for a country that interests you. Write down the details for a short presentation to the class. You can use the Web site listed below, consult a contemporary encyclopedia, or find another source by doing a Web search for the specific country in which you are interested.

www.cia.gov/library/publications/the-world-factbook/

CHAPTER 2

Immigration

TOPIC PREVIEW

Answer the following questions with a partner or your classmates.

1. What reasons might a person have for immigrating to a new country?

2. What challenges might immigrants face adjusting to a new culture? What personal qualities might people need to start life in a new culture?

3. Can immigration help the country from which the immigrants came? How?

An immigrant family looks across New York Harbor at the Statue of Liberty, 1930s.

VOCABULARY PREVIEW

CD 1, TR 8

A Read through the sentences below, which are missing vocabulary from the lecture. As you read, try to imagine which words would fit in the blanks. Then listen to the sentences and write the missing words in the blanks.

1. Sometimes people immigrate to a new country to escape political or religious _____ .

2. Rather than immigrants, the early _____ from Great Britain considered themselves _____ ; they had left home to settle new land for the mother country.

3. The so-called Great Immigration, which can be divided into three _____ , or time periods, began about 1830 and lasted till about 1930.

4. The Industrial Revolution, which began in the nineteenth century, caused _____ unemployment as machines replaced workers.

5. The _____ of farmland in Europe caused many people to immigrate to the United States, where there was an _____ of available land.

6. Land in the United States was plentiful and available when the country was _____ westward. In fact, the U.S. government offered free public land to _____ in 1862.

7. The failure of the Irish potato crop in the middle of the nineteenth century caused _____ starvation.

8. The first law that limited the number of immigrants coming from a certain part of the world was the Chinese Exclusion Act of 1882, but in 1965 strict _____ based on nationality were _____ .

9. This is the largest number of immigrants in history, although the _____ of the total population, 12.8 percent, has been larger in the past.

10. Strict anti-immigration laws at the state or federal level and _____ against employers who hire illegal immigrants could lead to a _____ in immigration to the United States.

B Check the spelling of the vocabulary words with your teacher. Discuss the meanings of these words and any other unfamiliar words in the sentences.

PREDICTIONS

Think about the questions in the Topic Preview on page 10 and the sentences you heard in the Vocabulary Preview. Write three questions that you think will be answered in the lecture. Share your questions with your classmates.

NOTETAKING PREPARATION

Recording Dates

Hearing dates accurately and writing them down in your notes correctly are very important, but sometimes it can be difficult because we usually say dates two numbers at a time. For example, 1776 is said as *seventeen seventy-six*, and 2010 is often said as *twenty ten*. A whole decade is given as a plural: the 1940s / the nineteen forties.

Another difficulty is that it is easy to confuse *teens* and *tens*. For *teens*, both syllables are stressed—FIF TEEN—with slightly more stress on the second syllable. For *tens*, only the first syllable is stressed—FIF ty.

CD 1, TR 9

A You will hear ten dates and phrases. As you listen, write each date or phrase in notetaking form in the spaces below.

1. _____   6. _____

2. _____   7. _____

3. _____   8. _____

4. _____   9. _____

5. _____   10. _____

Names of Countries and Peoples

Greece or Greek? To take accurate notes of a lecture that includes many names of countries and peoples, you must know the terms used for each of them. The following few guidelines may help you.

- The plural for most nationalities is formed by adding *-s*: *a Mexican, Mexicans*.
- Nationalities ending in *-ese* can be singular or plural: *a Vietnamese, the Vietnamese*.
- When a nationality adjective ends in *-sh* or *-ch*, add *the* to mean the people of those countries: *the French*; *the British*.

CD 1, TR 10

B Below is a list of countries and peoples that will be mentioned in the lecture. Fill in the missing words, then listen as the list is read and check your answers. Check the spelling with your teacher.

Country	People
1. France	the French
2. Germany	_____
3. _____	Scots or the Scottish
4. Ireland	_____

5. _____ the British or Britons

6. _____ Danes

7. _____ Norwegians

8. _____ Swedes

9. the Netherlands or Holland _____

10. Greece _____

11. _____ Italians

12. _____ the Spanish or Spaniards

13. _____ the Portuguese

14. China _____

15. _____ Filipinos

16. _____ Mexicans

17. India _____

18. _____ Russians

19. _____ Poles

20. Vietnam _____

C **Answer the following questions with a partner or your classmates.**

1. Which of the countries in the list in Exercise B are Scandinavian?

2. Which of the countries in the list in Exercise B are Southern European?

3. Which of the countries in the list in Exercise B are Eastern European countries?

D **Discourse Cues** **Number the following excerpts from the lecture from 1 to 5 in the order that you think you will probably hear them. Discuss with a partner or as a class the discourse cues that helped you figure out the order.**

_____ Now that we've talked about the historical situation, let's discuss the current situation with respect to immigration.

_____ Now that we know something about the numbers and origins of immigrants who came to the States during the Great Immigration, let's consider the reasons.

_____ Immigration declined somewhat after the Great Immigration.

_____ We'll begin our discussion today with the period of history called the Great Immigration.

_____ Last, it might be interesting to speculate on immigration in the future.

FIRST LISTENING

CD 1, TR 11

A Listen to the beginning of the lecture. Circle the set of notes below that best records the information you hear.

a.

```
Immigration
Early Britons
Settlers—no immig, mother country
   Dutch, French, Ger, Scot, Irish, Afr
   40% live in US spk Eng 1776
   Colonial period
   Immigration great in 1830
      1930 — reasons why great
      Decrease 1940
      1970 — US today
```

b.

```
Americans see nation of immigrants
Colonial peri
   Britons — settlers/colonists, not immig
         settle land for Gr Brit
   Dutch, French, Ger, Scot-Irish settlers
   African slaves
   independ from Gr Brit 1776
         40% not Brit, but maj. speak Eng
Great Immig 1830—1930
Reasons for Gr Immig
Decreased immig 1940—1970
Immig in US today
```

CD 1, TR 12

B Now listen to the whole lecture and take notes. Look at the lecturer's visual aids as you listen. These may help you understand parts of the lecture.

Subtopic 1: _____

Immigration 1830–1930

Subtopic 2: _____

Causes
1. Doubling of European population 1750–1850
2. Industrial Revolution—Unemployment
3. Land scarcity in Europe
4. Religious and political persecution
5. Natural disasters

Subtopic 3: _____

Decline
• Chinese Exclusion Act of 1882
• Great Depression of 1929
• World War II (1937–1945)

Subtopic 4: _____

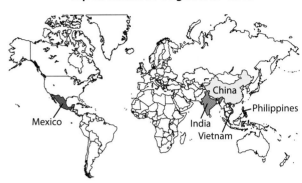

Top Countries of Origin 2000–2010

Canada

Mexico

China

Philippines

India

Vietnam

🔊 **SECOND LISTENING**
CD 1, TR 13

Listen to the lecture again and make your notes as complete as possible.

THIRD LISTENING

🔊 **Ⓐ** You will hear part of the lecture again. Listen and complete the notes by adding
CD 1, TR 14 the information from the box.

| ↑ | 1965 | 2000 | 12.8 | 3/4 | Eur | VN |

Immigr. _____–Nat. quotas elim & _____ imm. since then
- 2010 40M imm (_____% ttl pop)
  _____ legal
- lgst # in histry
- NOT _____; 58% Lat Am (_____–2010)
  1. Mex 12M
  2. China
  3. India
  4. Phili.
  5. _____

Ⓑ Compare your answers with a partner. Then compare the notes in **A** with the
notes you took for this part of the lecture.

ACCURACY CHECK

CD 1, TR 15

A Listen to the following questions, and write short answers. Use your notes. You will hear each question one time only.

1. _____
2. _____
3. _____
4. _____
5. _____
6. _____
7. _____
8. _____
9. _____
10. _____

B Check your answers with your teacher. If your score is less than 70 percent, you may need to listen to the lecture again and rewrite some of your notes.

ORAL SUMMARY

Use your notes to create an oral summary of the lecture with your partner. As you work together, add details to your notes that your partner included but you had missed.

DISCUSSION

Discuss the following questions with a classmate or in a small group.

1. How different would the United States culture, economy, or its politics be today if there had been no immigration after the year 1900?

2. When discussing the history of immigration in the United States, do you think it is right to use the term *immigrants* for black Africans brought to the United States as slaves? Why or why not?

3. What are some of the benefits of having immigrants in a country? What are some of the disadvantages? Give specific examples.

PRE-READING

The following Reading is about environmental refugees. Before you read, answer the following questions. Share your answers with a classmate.

1. Look up the word *refugee* in a dictionary. What is the difference between an immigrant and a refugee? Which of the immigrants in the lecture could be described as refugees?

2. What do you think the term *environmental refugee* means? What kinds of environmental problems could cause people to leave their home countries?

READING

Now read the article.

Climate Change Creating Millions of "Eco Refugees," UN Warns

Environmental problems around the world are creating a new category of people known as "environmental refugees," says the United Nations University—Institute for Environment and Human Security (UNU-EHS). What's more, the number of these refugees is growing rapidly. There are at least 20 million environmental refugees worldwide, the group says.

UNU-EHS predicts that by 2010 the number of environmental refugees could grow to 50 million. According to other estimates, there could be as many as 150 million by 2050. That's why nations and aid groups need to immediately recognize and help this new category of refugee, UNU-EHS says. But helping them first requires a clear definition of an environmental refugee. "How you define somebody can be an issue of life and death for them," said Anthony Oliver-Smith, a University of Florida anthropologist who is a member of the UN group.

Global Warming Refugees?

Environmental disasters like Hurricane Katrina in New Orleans can destroy the homes of millions of people in a moment. But many other people are displaced by gradual environmental changes. And these changes may be linked to climate change.

In China, the Gobi desert expands more than 10,000 square miles each year, forcing many farmers there to leave, the UNU-EHS reports. Thousands of miles away in Alaska about 200 villages are in serious danger due to rising sea levels. The entire Inupiat village of Shishmaref is planning to move 13.5 miles inland in the next four years to avoid rising waters.

"Human migrations are expected to increase as average global temperatures continue to rise and we experience rising sea levels, more severe weather disasters, and other impacts as a result," said Janet Sawin, a climate change expert.

Gobi desert, Central Asia

Shishmaref, Alaska

Long-term drought, or lack of rain, another possible effect of global warming, could also force people to leave increasingly dry lands. Some people, who in the past would leave during the dry season and then come back after it rained, may decide never to return.

Because many environmental changes are ultimately caused by humans, some experts say the term *environmental refugee* is misleading. "It tends to suggest that nature is at fault, when in fact humans are deeply implicated in the environmental changes that make life impossible in certain circumstances," Oliver-Smith said.

What's In a Name?

While victims of political conflict are entitled to food and shelter through government and aid groups, environmental refugees are not yet recognized by international law. Some have pointed out that environmental change may be just one of many factors that cause people to leave their homes. But Oliver-Smith disagrees. "An environmental issue may not be the only thing driving people away, but it may be the big one," he said.

The UN university experts are now working to establish terms to define people who have been displaced by environmental change. Once this new class of refugee is defined, the UN experts say, work can begin on providing them with aid. "Despite the seriousness of these trends, the issue of environmental refugees has received scant attention at the highest level," said Rhoda Margesson, foreign affairs analyst with the U.S. Congressional Research Service in Washington, D.C.

DISCUSSION

Discuss these questions with a classmate.

1. Make a list of the reasons for immigration described in the lecture and those described in the article. Are any of these reasons the same? In what ways?

2. How are today's environmental refugees different from the immigrants who came to the United States in the nineteenth and twentieth centuries?

3. Based on what you learned in the lecture and the article, do you think the number of immigrants to the United States will increase or decrease in the next 50 years? Why?

PURSUING THE TOPIC

Explore the topic of this chapter further by doing the following.

Watch the documentary *The Other Side of Immigration*, directed by Roy Germano, available online at the Web page below. Be prepared to discuss it with your classmates.

www.theothersideofimmigration.com/HOME.html

CHAPTER 3

Work in America

Discuss the following questions with a partner or your classmates.

1. What type of work do you do now or hope to do in the future?

2. In what types of jobs do workers provide a service rather than produce something?

3. In which country do you think a larger percentage of the workforce is engaged in agriculture, the United States or China? Why do you think so?

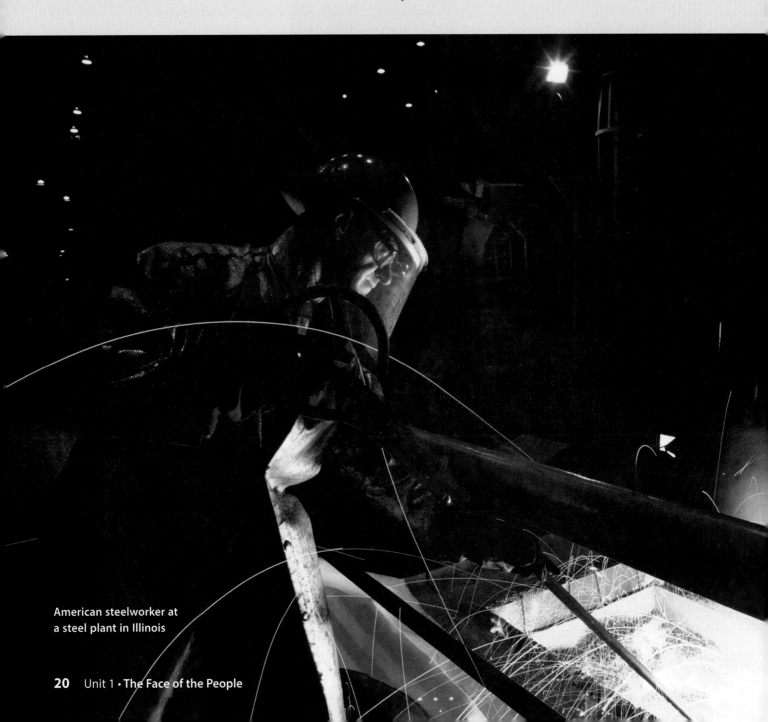

American steelworker at a steel plant in Illinois

VOCABULARY PREVIEW

CD 1, TR 16

A **Read through the sentences below, which are missing vocabulary from the lecture. As you read, try to imagine which words would fit in the blanks. Then listen to the sentences and write the missing words in the blanks.**

1. There was also a large _____ in the number of people working in _____, that is, in making, or manufacturing, things in factories.

2. While the number of people in agriculture and manufacturing industries went _____, the number of people in the services went _____ dramatically.

3. Over the years, child labor laws became much _____ and by 1999, it was _____ for anyone under 16 to work full-time in any of the 50 states.

4. In 1900, only 19 percent of women were _____; in 2010, almost 73 percent of women were holding _____ jobs.

5. For much of the twentieth century, U.S. workers saw rising _____, increased benefits like Social _____ and health insurance, and better working conditions.

6. While the productivity of the U.S. _____ has continued to increase since the 1970s, wages for the working class have not increased.

7. Let me give you some statistics that may help you understand the impact of _____ wages and high _____.

8. Labor _____, which protect workers' rights, have become weaker in the past decades.

9. Lack of regulation of financial institutions has led to very _____ investments, which have led to loss of jobs, lost _____, and loss of homes.

10. "Cautious _____" about the U.S. economy seems to be the watchword of the day in newspapers and magazine articles about the economy at this time.

B **Check the spelling of the vocabulary words with your teacher. Discuss the meanings of these words and any other unfamiliar words in the sentences.**

PREDICTIONS

Think about the questions in the Topic Preview on page 20 and the sentences you heard in the Vocabulary Preview. Write three questions that you think will be answered in the lecture. Share your questions with your classmates.

NOTETAKING PREPARATION

Using Symbols and Abbreviations 1

When you take notes on a lecture, you will not have time to write down all the important information. That is why good notetakers use symbols and abbreviations. Try these tips.

Use conventional symbols

& or +	and
=	equals; is the same as
≠	not; not the same as
>;<	more than; less than
@	at
↑	go up; increase
↓	go down; decrease
"	ditto (the same as above)

Use conventional abbreviations

cent.	century
ex	example
info	information
intro	introduction
max	maximum
min	minimum
psych	psychology; psychological
stats	statistics

Use the first syllable or the first syllable + the first letter of the second syllable

educ	education	subj	subject
lect	lecture	transp	transportation subject
pres	president		

Make up your own abbreviations

Lectures will usually include words for which you cannot use conventional symbols and abbreviations. Most lectures will also have words that are unique to the topic of the lecture. In such cases, make up your own abbreviations. Just be sure to create abbreviations that will help you remember the complete words when you go back and read your notes.

CD 1, TR 17

A **Listen to the statements from the lecture. Circle the notes that best use symbols and abbreviations to record what you hear.**

1. a. large peop work in industry
   b. # of people in indus ↓ a lot
   c. many people lost jobs

2. a. > 16: illeg to wk full time
   b. < 60 illegal to work in 50 sts
   c. in 50 sts: >16 illegal to work

3. a. end of 20th C.: 3% on farms
   b. end cent.: 3% wkd on farms
   c. end of century: 30% of workers on farms

B Write abbreviations for the following terms used in the lecture. Use abbreviations that you will understand when you read your notes a few days or a few weeks later.

Term	Abbreviation
1. agriculture	_____
2. the service sector	_____
3. child labor	_____
4. stagnant wages and high unemployment	_____
5. health insurance	_____
6. income	_____
7. outsourcing and advanced technology	_____
8. lower wages and loss of jobs	_____
9. lack of regulation	_____
10. conservative	_____
11. liberal	_____
12. polarized	_____

C Cover the terms on the left. With a partner, take turns saying the terms that your abbreviations stand for.

D Discourse Cues Number the following excerpts from the lecture from 1 to 5 in the order that you think you will probably hear them. Discuss with a partner or as a class the discourse cues that helped you figure out the order.

_____ Finally, let's take a look at some of the possible reasons for the current situation.

_____ OK, now let's take a look at how the U.S. workforce is doing today.

_____ First, we'll take a historical look at work in America.

_____ We're going to take a look at work in the United States today in different ways.

_____ Let's get back to the changes in the U.S. workforce in the last century or so before we move on to the current situation.

FIRST LISTENING

CD 1, TR 18

Listen to the lecture and take notes. Look at the lecturer's visual aids as you listen. These may help you understand parts of the lecture.

Introduction

> **Work in America**
>
> Introduction
>
> Changes – 1900 to 2010
> U.S. workers today
> The current economic situation
> The role of the government

Subtopic 1: _____

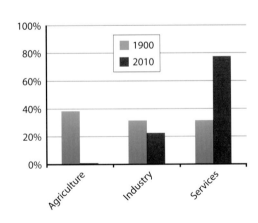

Subtopic 2: _____

U.S. Workers Today

Most of Twentieth Century
- Rising wages
- Increased benefits
- Better working conditions

Today
- Productivity up, but not wages
- High unemployment

Subtopic 3: _____

Current Economic Situation

Reasons
- Agriculture mechanized
- Outsourcing
- Advances in technology
- Weaker labor unions

Subtopic 4: _____

Role of the Government

Government Policy
- Tax cuts vs. tax increases
- More regulation of business vs. less regulation
- Liberals and conservatives are polarized

SECOND LISTENING

Listen to the lecture again and make your notes as complete as possible.

THIRD LISTENING

A You will hear part of the lecture again. Listen and complete the notes by adding the information from the box.

| " | ↑ | + | mid | Stats | WWII | 33% |

U.S. wrkfrce today

_____ Produc since 1970, but wrking cl wages same

_____ Unempl

_____

After _____: poor child 50% _____ class as adult

1980: _____ child 40% " " " "

2012: " " _____ " " " "

B Compare your answers with a partner. Then compare the notes in **A** with the notes you took for this part of the lecture.

ACCURACY CHECK

CD 1, TR 21

A Listen to the following questions, and write short answers. Use your notes. You will hear each question one time only.

1. _____
2. _____
3. _____
4. _____
5. _____
6. _____
7. _____
8. _____
9. _____
10. _____

B Check your answers with your teacher. If your score is less than 70 percent, you may need to listen to the lecture again and rewrite some of your notes.

ORAL SUMMARY

Use your notes to create an oral summary of the lecture with your partner. As you work together, add details to your notes that your partner included but you had missed.

DISCUSSION

Discuss the following questions with a classmate or in a small group.

1. The lecture doesn't discuss solutions to problems in the economy. What solutions can you offer?

2. How do you think the American economy might change in the next 10 years?

3. What advantages and disadvantages are there in globalization, where the world's economies are interconnected through outsourcing and global markets?

PRE-READING

The following Reading is about Zhejiang Province in China. Before you read, answer the following questions. Share your answers with a classmate.

1. What sector of the economy do you think employs the largest percentage of workers in China?

2. Look at the title of the article. What is a *boomtown*? What do you think an *instant city* is?

READING

Now read the article.

Boomtowns: China's Instant Cities

For the past 30 years, China's economy has averaged nearly 10 percent growth per year. This rapid growth rate is at least partially the result of one of the largest population movements in history: An estimated 140 million rural Chinese have already left their homes, and another 45 million are expected to join the urban workforce in the next five years. Most have gone to factory towns along the coast. However, in recent years more have moved to cities in the middle of the country, where there's less competition for jobs.

One of these cities is Wenzhou. The Wenzhou airport bookstore sells a book titled *Actually, You Don't Understand the Wenzhou People*. It shares a shelf with *The Collected Secrets of How Wenzhou People Make Money*. For the Chinese, this part of Zhejiang Province has become a source of fascination. Recently, Wenzhou's *Fortune Weekly* conducted a study of local millionaires. One question was: If forced to choose between your business and your family, which would it be? Sixty percent chose business.

Throughout history, difficult circumstances helped create the Wenzhou business tradition. The region is dry and not easy to farm, and the mountains make travel challenging. With few options, Wenzhou natives turned to the sea. By the end of the seventeenth century, they had developed a strong trading culture. But in 1949, the communists came to power and cut off overseas trade, as well as most private business. Even in the early 1980s, when China introduced free-market reforms, Wenzhou started with definite disadvantages. The people from Wenzhou did not have the education of people in Beijing, and they didn't attract the foreign investment of Shanghai.

But Wenzhou had something very valuable: native instinct. Families opened small workshops, often with fewer than a dozen workers, and they produced simple goods. Over time, workshops grew into factories, and Wenzhou began to dominate certain low-tech industries. Today, one-quarter of all shoes bought in China come from Wenzhou. The city makes 70 percent of the world's cigarette lighters.

The Wenzhou Model spread throughout southern Zhejiang Province, where an amazing range of products is manufactured. In the city of Qiaotou, population 64,000, 380 local factories produce more than 70 percent of the buttons for clothes made in China. The region also produces one-third of the world's socks and 40 percent of the world's neckties.

Everything is sold in a town in Zhejiang Province called Yiwu. Yiwu is in the middle of nowhere, a hundred miles from the coast, but traders come from all over the world to buy. The China Yiwu International Trade City, a local mall, has more than 30,000 shops—if you spend one minute at each one, eight hours a day, you'll leave two months later.

One of the 30,000 shops in Yiwu market

Although nearly 80 percent of all Zhejiang business owners have a formal education of only eight years or fewer, the province has become the richest in China by most measures. The incomes for both rural and urban residents are the highest of any Chinese province (this excludes specially administered cities such as Shanghai and Beijing). Zhejiang reflects China's economic miracle: a poor, mostly rural nation that has somehow become the world's most productive factory center.

DISCUSSION

Discuss these questions with a classmate.

1. What information from the lecture was exemplified in the article?

2. Based on the article and what you learned from the lecture, what are the similarities between China today and the United States in 1900?

3. Compare the economic situation in China as explained in the article to the economic situation in the United States today as explained in the lecture. Which economy do you think is likely to do better over the long term? Why?

PURSUING THE TOPIC

Explore the topic of this chapter further by doing the following.

The Web site for the U.S. Bureau of Labor Statistics has a large amount of current information about all aspects of employment in the United States. Individually or with a partner, choose a topic that interests you and read about it. Write up the details for a short presentation to the class.

www.bls.gov

UNIT 1 VIDEO
Cowboys in North America

TOPIC PREVIEW

Answer the following questions with a partner.

1. What do you know about the history of the American cowboy?

2. What do you think the working life of a cowboy is or was like?

3. Do you think there are many cowboys in America today? Why or why not?

VOCABULARY PREVIEW

A Read the definitions of these key words and phrases that you will hear during the video.

hold on to their culture keep their traditions and lifestyle

ranches large areas of land where cows and horses are raised and where the owner, workers, and their families live

exposed to forced to experience, usually something bad like bad weather

gear equipment; clothes and tools needed for a particular job, sport, or activity

the outdoors places outside and away from the house; in the natural world

50 below an outside temperature of 50 degrees below zero Fahrenheit (-50°F)

don't mind are not bothered by or not worried about

child-bearing age between approximately age 13 and 50, when a woman is able to have a baby

duties responsibilities

a vanishing breed types or groups of people who are starting to disappear

B Work with a partner and write vocabulary from **A** in the blanks in the sentences.

1. Families living on these _____ really _____ the difficulties of this lifestyle.

2. Sometimes women work as cowboys, especially when they are past _____.

3. To work as a cowboy, one has to love _____.

4. Even the children have many _____ around the ranch.

5. These men and women can be _____ temperatures as low as _____.

6. Cowboys have been able to _____ and not become _____.

7. A cowboy's _____ includes a big hat, pointed boots, and a rope, among other things.

VIEWING

⌨ FIRST VIEWING

Watch the video, and then compare your first impressions with a partner. Talk about what you remember, what surprised you, and what interested you.

⌨ SECOND VIEWING

Watch the video again. Listen for the missing words and write them in the blanks.

1. The cowboy basically breaks into _____ different types.

2. These people have been able to hold on to their culture because they love the _____.

3. So, you know a typical _____ guy at one of these ranches makes anywhere from eight to twelve hundred dollars a _____.

4. So, when you do the _____ on it, it's, you know, three to four dollars an hour.

5. I mean, what it takes to cowboy is good _____ skills, skill with a rope, and a real understanding on how to work _____ on a horse.

6. But still, the cheapest way to raise cattle is by _____ them grass, and you're not going to do that on a four-wheeler on 1.3 _____ acres.

💻 THIRD VIEWING

Complete these notes as you watch the video. Write only important words, not full sentences, and abbreviate common words.

1) _____ types of cb

2) hold on to _____
   – love their _____
   – earn _____
   – get housing and _____
   – work _____ hrs a _____

3) Gear and skills
   – understand _____
   – love _____
   but cold – sometimes = 50 _____

4) Women as cbs – not _____
   – usu young or _____
   – kids _____

5) Ppl predict cbs a _____
   – but still cheapest way _____

AFTER VIEWING

ORAL SUMMARY

Use your notes to create an oral summary of the video with your partner. As you work together, add details to your notes that your partner included but you had missed.

DISCUSSION

Discuss the following questions with a classmate or in a small group.

1. Based on what you learned about a cowboy's working life in America today, would you like to be a cowboy? Why or why not?

2. According to the speaker, the cowboy has been around for over 150 years in America but is not a "vanishing breed." What are some cultures and jobs that have vanished in that time period and why?

3. Do you think there will always be a need for cowboys in the United States? Why or why not?

The American Character

Head of Abraham Lincoln being
sculpted at Mount Rushmore,
South Dakota, ca 1934

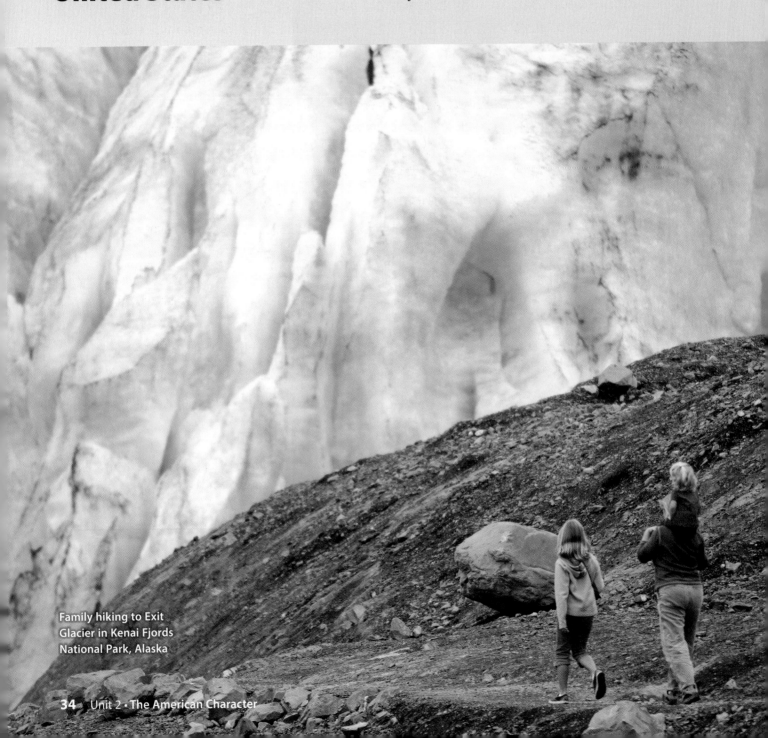

CHAPTER 4

Family in the United States

TOPIC PREVIEW

Discuss the following questions with a partner or your classmates.

1. How would you describe a typical U.S. family?

2. Are single-parent families common in your culture?

3. Is it common for parents in your culture to leave children in day care while they are away at work?

Family hiking to Exit Glacier in Kenai Fjords National Park, Alaska

VOCABULARY PREVIEW

CD 2, TR 1

A Read through the sentences below, which are missing vocabulary from the lecture. As you read, try to imagine which words would fit in the blanks. Then listen to the sentences and write the missing words in the blanks.

1. Although many social scientists are concerned about the decrease in marriage and its possible negative effects on the family, others say it is wrong to assume that marriage in the United States is "on the _____."

2. In any society, economic and cultural elements _____ with each other and bring _____ change.

3. This was the period after World War II, a period _____ by a very strong economy, a rising _____ of living, and a growing middle class.

4. The typical _____ of the family in these years was the traditional one: a married couple with children.

5. Culturally, three characteristics stand out in this period: _____ to social norms, greater male domination of the family than in the later periods, and very clear gender roles.

6. The women's liberation movement was an _____ of the struggle for civil rights.

7. Women's liberation challenged _____ against women in the home, in the work place, and in society in general.

8. Three movements—the sexual revolution, women's liberation, and the antiwar movement—were typical of the _____ nature of these decades.

9. With more women having careers and making money, there was less economic pressure for them to stay in an _____ marriage.

10. Many experts _____ that children have paid a high price for the social changes that took place in the second period.

B Check the spelling of the vocabulary words with your teacher. Discuss the meanings of these words and any other unfamiliar words in the sentences.

PREDICTIONS

Think about the questions in the Topic Preview on page 34 and the sentences you heard in the Vocabulary Preview. Write three questions that you think will be answered in the lecture. Share your questions with your classmates.

NOTETAKING PREPARATION

Listening for Key Content Words

Use key words to write down the essential information in a lecture. It is neither possible nor necessary to write every word you hear. Here are some tips for choosing key words.

- Concentrate on content words: nouns, verbs, adjectives, and adverbs.
- Choose the most important words to convey the meaning in the fewest words possible. For example, you hear

    Culturally, three characteristics stand out in this period: conformity to social norms, greater male domination of the family than in the later periods, and very clear gender roles, that is, clear and separate roles for men and women at home and at work.

    You write

    3 characteristics: social conformity, male domination & clear gender roles @ home & work

- You may also choose to put some information in your own words. For example, instead of writing conformity to social norms, you might write social conformity.

A Practice reducing information to key words as you listen to sentences from the lecture. Then compare what you wrote with a classmate.

CD 2, TR 2

1. _____

2. _____

3. _____

B Discourse Cues Number the following excerpts from the lecture from 1 to 5 in the order that you think you will probably hear them. Discuss with a partner or as a class the discourse cues that helped you figure out the order.

_____ The third period is harder to see because we are living in this period now.

_____ So, let's begin with the first period, the mid-1940s to the mid-1960s.

_____ In addition to the cultural changes during this period of individualism, there were also economic changes that affected families.

_____ The second period that I want to talk about today, the period of individualism, lasted from the mid-1960s to the mid-1980s.

_____ Let me begin today's lecture by saying that many people today are concerned about the decline in the number of people who are married in the United States.

FIRST LISTENING

CD 2, TR 3

A Listen to the beginning of the lecture. Circle the set of notes below that best records the information you hear.

a.

> Fewer peopl married in US
>
> | | 1960 | today |
> |---|---|---|
> | whts | 74% | 55% |
> | hisp. | 72% | 48% |
> | blks | 61% | 31% |
> | 18-24 | 45% | 9% |
>
> Cult. changes – diff. ideas marr & fam
>   econ + cult = change
>   views ch over time
> 3 time peri. (Soc. Barbra Dafoe Whitehead)
>   1. mid–40s to mid–60s: trad. fam
>   2. mid–60s to mid–80s: individualism
>   3. present: new fam

b.

> ↓ marriage in US
>   55–74% whts
>   48–72% hisp
>   31–61% blks
>   45–9% young
> Neg. impact on fam?
> Diff. ideas about marr & fam?
> Change happening in US
>   Way Am see fam
>   How views have changed
>   ex: tradt fam, individ, new fam

CD 2, TR 4

B Now listen to the whole lecture and take notes. Look at the lecturer's visual aids as you listen. These may help you understand parts of the lecture.

Subtopic 1: <u>1940s–1960s: Traditional Family</u>

> **Traditional Family**
> - Conformity to social roles
> - Male domination
> - Clear gender roles

Subtopic 2: <u>1960s–1980s: Individualism</u>

> **Individualism**
>
> **Cultural developments**
> - Focus on career and work
> - Self-expression/fulfillment
>
> **Economic changes**
> - Women work outside the home

Chapter 4 · **Family in the United States**   37

Subtopic 3: _Present: The New Family_

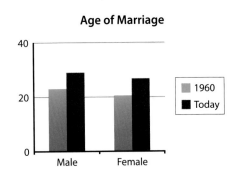

Age of Marriage

40

20

0

Male   Female

1960
Today

🔊
CD 2, TR 5

SECOND LISTENING

Listen to the lecture again and make your notes as complete as possible.

THIRD LISTENING

🔊
CD 2, TR 6

A You will hear part of the lecture again. Listen and complete the notes by adding the information from the box.

| charac | div | mid | soc | WWII | + | @ |

mid 1940s – mid 1960s = Tradtl Fam
    After _____ + Econ
      ↑ standard of liv, ↑ _____ class
• Fam = marr couple + child: husb work, wife _____ home
• low _____ rate, + birth rate
• 3 cult _____
    1. _____ conformity
    2. _____ male domination of fam
    3. Clear gender roles

B Compare your answers with a partner. Then compare the notes in **A** with the notes you took for this part of the lecture.

ACCURACY CHECK

CD 2, TR 7

A Listen to the following questions, and write short answers. Use your notes. You will hear each question one time only.

1. _____

2. _____

3. _____

4. _____

5. _____

6. _____

7. _____

8. _____

9. _____

10. _____

B Check your answers with your teacher. If your score is less than 70 percent, you may need to listen to the lecture again and rewrite some of your notes.

ORAL SUMMARY

Use your notes to create an oral summary of the lecture with your partner. As you work together, add details to your notes that your partner included but you had missed.

DISCUSSION

Discuss the following statements with a classmate or in a small group.

1. What similarities are there between what you've learned about typical U.S. families and families in your culture?

2. What effects have economic and cultural changes in the last 20 years or so had on the family in your culture?

3. Is divorce always a bad idea? Can it ever have positive consequences for the family?

PRE-READING

The following Reading is about changes in family size in Brazil. Before you read, answer the following questions. Share your answers with a classmate.

1. Was there a women's movement in your country? If so, how was that movement similar to the women's movement in the 1970s in the United States?

2. Look at the title of the article. What does "female empowerment" mean? How do you think changes in family size might be related to female empowerment?

READING

Now read the article.

Female Empowerment in Brazil and its Effect on the Fertility Rate

Eighty-eight-year-old Brazilian Dona Maria Ribeiro de Carvalho had just finished telling me about her 16 pregnancies. Then she looked at José Alberto, her oldest son, who had come for a Sunday visit. "With the number of children I had," Dona Maria said, "I should have more than a hundred grandchildren right now."

Dona Maria's son José Alberto Carvalho, one of the most important Brazilian demographers of the past 50 years, smiled. He knew the total number of grandchildren, of course: 26. For much of his working life, he has been studying the remarkable Brazilian demographic phenomenon that is illustrated by his own family, which within two generations had crashed its fertility rate to 2.36 children per family, close to the national average of 1.9.

That new Brazilian fertility rate is below replacement level—the level at which a population replaces itself. It is lower than the two-children-per-woman fertility rate in the United States. And it's not simply wealthy and professional women who have stopped having multiple children in Brazil—every class and region of Brazil has experienced a drop.

This sudden fertility drop is not just a Brazilian phenomenon. Close to half the world's population lives in countries where the fertility rates have fallen to below replacement rate, just over two children per

family. However, what has happened in Brazil since the 1960s provides a fascinating case study.

"What took 120 years in England took 40 years here," Carvalho told me one day. "Something *happened*." At that moment he was talking about what happened in São Vicente de Minas, the town of his childhood, where nobody under 45 has large families anymore. But he could have been describing the entire female population of Brazil. For although there are many reasons Brazil's fertility rate has dropped so far and so fast, central to them all are Brazil's women.

Brazilian women's overall position in society was deeply affected by the women's movement of the 1970s and '80s. Today, Brazil is led by its first female president, Dilma Rousseff; during the campaign, one of Rousseff's strongest competitors was a female senator. Brazil has high-ranking female military officers, special police stations run by and for women, and the world's most famous female soccer player, the one-name-only Marta.

Aníbal Faúndes, a Chilean professor who immigrated years ago to Brazil and has helped lead national studies of reproductive health, explains what he regards as a primary reason for the changes in birthrate in his adopted country. "The fertility rate dropped because women decided they didn't

Brazilians are now having much smaller families.

want more children," he said. "Brazilian women are tremendously strong."

Keeping the family small is what Brazilian women of all ages now seem to expect of themselves—and what contemporary Brazil, in turn, appears to expect from them. "Look at the apartments," said a 31-year-old Rio de Janeiro marketing executive named Andiara Petterle. "They're designed for a maximum of four people. Two bedrooms. In the supermarkets, even the labels on frozen foods—always for four people."

The company Petterle founded specializes in sales research on Brazilian women, whose buying habits and life priorities seem to have changed completely in the years since Petterle was born. It wasn't until 1977, she reminded me, that the nation legalized divorce. "We've changed so fast," she said. "We've found that for many young women, their first priority now is their education. The second is their profession. And the third is children and a stable relationship."

DISCUSSION

Discuss these questions with a classmate.

1. What are some of the similarities in how Brazilian and American attitudes toward the family have changed over time?

2. How did the women's movement of the 1970s and 1980s affect Brazilian society? Compare its impact to the impact of the women's movement on American culture described in the lecture.

3. In what ways are Brazilian families today similar to American families? How are they different?

PURSUING THE TOPIC

Explore the topic of this chapter further by doing the following.

The Web site for the United States Census Bureau has a large amount of information about American families. Individually or with a partner, research the most recent statistical information available on family size, relationships, and living arrangements. Write up the details for a short presentation to the class.

www.census.gov/hhes/families/

CHAPTER 5

Religion

TOPIC PREVIEW

Discuss the following questions with a partner or your classmates.

1. What do you think the expression "freedom of religion" means?

2. Do people in your culture practice many different religions in your culture?

3. In what country other than the United States do you think you might find all of these religions: Hinduism, Islam, Sikhism, Christianity, Judaism, Jainism, Zoroastrianism, and Buddhism?

Hindus pray at the Ganges river, India, near a statue of Shiva.

VOCABULARY PREVIEW

CD 2, TR 8

A Read through the sentences below, which are missing vocabulary from the lecture. As you read, try to imagine which words would fit in the blanks. Then listen to the sentences and write the missing words in the blanks.

1. These churches generally represent the two major Christian traditions, Catholic and Protestant, but often include several different Protestant _____.

2. Larger towns and big cities will also have other places of _____ including synagogues, mosques, and temples representing other religious traditions.

3. The U.S. government cannot ask for information on religious _____ in any official capacity, for example, on the census.

4. Statistical information must be gathered from _____ of the population done by nongovernmental agencies or from organizational reports from religious groups themselves.

5. A 2009 Gallup _____ asked, "Is religion an important part of your life?"

6. Most writers and scholars agree that Europeans are generally more _____ than Americans.

7. They may believe in God, but they _____ to stay away from religious _____ except on certain formal occasions like weddings, baptisms, and funerals and a few very important religious days.

8. It's important to remember that freedom of worship is guaranteed by the First _____ to the Constitution, which also establishes the separation of church and state.

9. Recently, however, there has been a _____ toward an increase in the influence of religion on American political life.

10. Although religion in America seemed to be in decline during most of the last century, in the 1970s, there was a religious _____ that surprised many people.

B Check the spelling of the vocabulary words with your teacher. Discuss the meanings of these words and any other unfamiliar words in the sentences.

PREDICTIONS

Think about the questions in the Topic Preview on page 42 and the sentences you heard in the Vocabulary Preview. Write three questions that you think will be answered in the lecture. Share your questions with your classmates.

NOTETAKING PREPARATION

Using Indentation to Organize Notes 1

Organizing your notes in a visual pattern will help you understand the relationship between the main ideas and the details or examples that support those ideas.

One way to organize your notes visually is by writing a main idea and then indenting the details and indicating them with bullets. Here are two examples.

Estimating people in diff. religions difficult
- U.S. govt can't ask for rel affiliation
- Statistics come from nongov surveys and reports

2007 survey gives % by rel
- 78% Christian
  - 51% Cath
  - 24% . . .
- 1.7% . . .
- 0.7% Budd
- 0.6% . . .
- 0.4% Hindu

A The following are lines of notes from a lecture titled "Effective Notetaking." Find three main ideas and circle them.

Do assigned rdg in prep

Fix notes as necess

Use symbols & abbrevs

After lecture

Put a ? for missed info

Bring ntbook & sharp pencils or pens

While notetaking

Ask prof ?s if nec

Before class

Be on time & find good seat

Review notes asap

Chk notes with classmate

B Now find three supporting details for each main idea. Draw lines from the details to the main idea they support.

C Using your ideas from **A**, write an outline of the lecture "Effective Notetaking."
Use indentation and bullets for the supporting details.

Effective Notetaking

D Discourse Cues Number the following excerpts from the lecture from 1 to 5 in
the order that you think you will probably hear them. Discuss with a partner or
as a class the discourse cues that helped you figure out the order.

_____ Now let's look at two major ways that religion in the United States differs from religion
in other modernized Western nations.

_____ Let's start today with facts and figures.

_____ One major survey conducted in 2007 reported that 78 percent of Americans identified
themselves as Christians.

_____ Finally, I'd like to briefly focus on religious diversity in the States.

_____ To sum up, then, the importance of religion and belonging to a church or religious
organization seem greater to Americans than to Europeans.

FIRST LISTENING

CD 2, TR 9

A Listen to the beginning of the lecture. Circle the set of notes below that best records the information you hear.

a.

> Relig in US complic
> - not understood by peop other count.
>   - know Am cult fr TV, film, video
>   - don't show imp of relig in US
> - sm towns many dif churches
>   - Chrisian: Cath & Protest (sev. dif)
> - lg towns & cities also synag., mosques, temples =other rel trad
> - people dif count. & relig immigr to US
>   - lg numb. dif relig
> 1 Facts & figures var relig groups in US
> 2 Comp US w other mod W nations
> 3 Imp of rel esp ↑ relig US polit recent yrs
> 4 Incr diversity of relig in US

b.

> Religion in U.S.
> - Compl topic misunderst bec other cults exposed to Am cult thru TV, film video on Internet
> - Internt visit to sm towns surprised bec Cath & Protest church (diff denom) & lg towns synag., mosque, temples
> - Peopl many diff countries & rel backg immig not surprised many dif rel US
> - Talk about today: 1st Facts and fig. var rel groups, 2nd comp US-modern West nat, 3rd import of rel increase in US polit, final increase diver rel in US

CD 2, TR 10

B Now listen to the whole lecture and take notes. Look at the lecturer's visual aids as you listen. These may help you understand parts of the lecture.

Subtopic 1: _____

Americans' Religious Affiliation, 2007

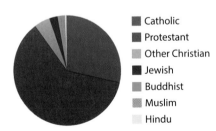

- Catholic
- Protestant
- Other Christian
- Jewish
- Buddhist
- Muslim
- Hindu

Subtopic 2: _____

Is religion an important part of
your life?

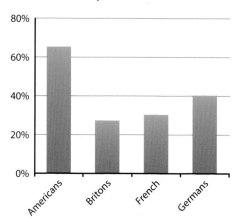

Subtopic 3: _____

**Rise of the Religious Right
(1970–present)**
- Oppose abortion
- Favor prayer in schools

Subtopic 4: _____

> **Religious Diversity**
> ▪ 1965: Immigration quotas eliminated
>   More religious diversity
> ▪ Work of Harvard professor Diana Eck
>
> **The Future**

CD 2, TR 11

🔊 SECOND LISTENING

Listen to the lecture again and make your notes as complete as possible.

THIRD LISTENING

CD 2, TR 12

🔊 **A** You will hear part of the lecture again. Listen and complete the notes by adding the information from the box.

Eur	free	indirect	influ	sep	&	ex.

Modrn, _____ nat.

   no sep of rel _____ govt.

US

    _____ of rel — 1st Amend to Const.

    _____ of church & state

    _____ rel not part of govt or pub schools

   Rel. beliefs, values _____ pol & ed,

     but _____ influ

B Compare your answers with a partner. Then compare the notes in **A** with the notes you took for this part of the lecture.

ACCURACY CHECK

CD 2, TR 13

A Listen to the following questions, and write short answers. Use your notes. You will hear each question one time only.

1. _____
2. _____
3. _____
4. _____
5. _____
6. _____
7. _____
8. _____
9. _____
10. _____

B Check your answers with your teacher. If your score is less than 70 percent, you may need to listen to the lecture again and rewrite some of your notes.

ORAL SUMMARY

Use your notes to create an oral summary of the lecture with your partner. As you work together, add details to your notes that your partner included but you had missed.

DISCUSSION

Discuss the following statements with a classmate or in a small group.

1. Do you believe that religious freedom is always a good thing? Why?

2. Should religion and government be totally separate? Why or why not?

3. Why might it be good for people learn about other people's religions?

PRE-READING

The following Reading is about religious beliefs around the world. Before you read, answer the following questions. Share your answers with a classmate.

1. What are the major religions in your country of origin? Are most people in your country religious?

2. Which areas of the world do you think have the highest number of people who are nonreligious or do not believe in God? Do you think there is a difference between someone who is nonreligious and an atheist who does not believe in God?

READING

Now read the article.

The Geography of Religion

The meaning of *religious belief* varies in different places, among different people. In general, *religion* refers to a set of beliefs and practices about what is sacred or spiritual—beliefs and practices held in common by a group. Religion usually involves beliefs about the origin and meaning of the world and of human life as well as guidelines for moral behavior.

Counting Adherents

There are many ways to approach the geography of religion, the simplest being to count numbers of believers by location. The data here came from the World Christian Database (WCD), which, despite its name, tracks data on hundreds of world religions in 238 political entities.

An *atheist* is someone who actively claims disbelief in the existence of God or any other deity. *Nonreligious* is a broader category that includes people who do not have a religion and also includes those who aren't opposed to religion, but who aren't interested in the question. Not surprisingly, the only country with no atheists or nonreligious citizens at all is Vatican City—home of the Roman Catholic Church. Afghanistan is next with a 99 percent Muslim population and a 99.99 percent religious-believer rate. Some other countries with at least a 99.90 percent religious-believer rate are: Bhutan (Buddhism); Bangladesh, Chad, Pakistan, and Somalia (Islam); Botswana, Burundi, and Kenya (Christianity).

There are very few countries in which more than 10 percent of the population claims to be atheist. They include North Korea (15.6 percent) and Sweden (11.7 percent). When you add the nonreligious and atheist populations together, however,

The holy Kaaba in Mecca, Saudi Arabia

the list of countries with significant percentages of nonbelievers grows. Here is a sampling of countries by region with nonbeliever populations of over 15 percent:

The Far East
North Korea (71.3%)
Mainland China (49.8%)

Central Asia
Mongolia (39.1%)
Kazakhstan (35.7%)
Kyrgyzstan (27.4%)

Eastern Europe
Czech Republic (35.6%)
Estonia (34.4%)
Russia (32.1%)

South America and the Caribbean
Uruguay (32.8%)
Cuba (24.5%)

Western Europe
Sweden (29.8%)
Netherlands (20.8%)
Germany (20.4%)

Australasia
New Zealand (21.4%)
Australia (16.9%)

The Problem of Numbers

The vast majority of the world's people—almost 86 percent, according to the WCD—hold some sort of religious belief. However, exact information about religious belief is among the hardest sociological data to collect. Religions count their members in a variety of ways, making comparisons difficult. Some include only those who regularly attend religious services; others count all known members, whether they attend services or not. Some count children from birth; others require some sort of ceremony before counting people as members. Polls, such as those collected by the Association of Religious Data Archives or the Pew Forum on Religion & Public Life, are frequently used to count believers, but results can vary widely.

Other approaches to understanding religion through geography include looking at sacred places and examining why some points on a map are considered so special to one or more religions that they become destinations for pilgrims. Another approach is to ask what direct physical impact a religion has had on a particular place: for example, cathedrals in Europe or the use of less-modern technology in Amish farming practices in North America.

DISCUSSION

Discuss these questions with a classmate.

1. What ideas presented in the lecture are given some support by information in the article?

2. Why is it difficult to collect exact data on people's religious beliefs, according to the lecture and the article? Make a list.

3. Look at the list of countries by region in the article. Using information from the lecture and your own ideas, can you think of reasons why these particular places might have so many nonbelievers?

PURSUING THE TOPIC

Explore the topic of this chapter further by doing the following.

Read an online interview with Professor Diana Eck in which she discusses her book, *A New Religious America: How a Christian Country Has Become the World's Most Religiously Diverse Nation.* Take notes and be prepared to discuss what you learned with your classmates.

www.pbs.org/wnet/religionandethics/episodes/april-26-2002/diana-eck-extended-interview/11617/

TOPIC PREVIEW

**Discuss the following questions with a
partner or your classmates.**

1. Have you been to a big American wedding?
   What was it like? Are weddings in your
   culture similar?

2. How do you think a couple in the United
   States would celebrate the birth of
   their baby?

3. What are some rituals people might carry
   out after the death of a loved one?

Wedding on a glacier!
Tongass National
Forest, Alaska

VOCABULARY PREVIEW

CD 2, TR 14

A Read through the sentences below, which are missing vocabulary from the lecture. As you read, try to imagine which words would fit in the blanks. Then listen to the sentences and write the missing words in the blanks.

1. Customs vary so much from culture to culture that it's often _____ for someone trying to understand the traditions and customs of a new place.

2. The birth of a baby is a _____ occasion in most families and is celebrated in some way or another.

3. Traditionally, Christian babies are _____ in a ceremony involving washing the baby's head with water.

4. The traditional reception that follows the ceremony can be as simple as cookies and punch in the house of worship where the ceremony took place or as _____ as a large sit-down dinner at a local hotel.

5. Traditionally, most wedding ceremonies have been _____ in houses of worship.

6. All traditions and religions have to cope with one basic issue: how to deal with the body of the _____ person.

7. Some religions such as Judaism and Islam require that the body be very quickly _____, or put into the ground.

8. This event, sometimes called a _____, usually takes place at a funeral home for a day or two before the funeral ceremony.

9. At the _____, it is customary for a religious leader to speak some words of comfort to the friends and family of the deceased. In addition, a _____ is usually given by someone close to the deceased person.

10. If the body is _____, the ashes are placed in a special jar, called an urn.

B Check the spelling of the vocabulary words with your teacher. Discuss the meanings of these words and any other unfamiliar words in the sentences.

PREDICTIONS

Think about the questions in the Topic Preview on page 52 and the sentences you heard in the Vocabulary Preview. Write three questions that you think will be answered in the lecture. Share your questions with your classmates.

NOTETAKING PREPARATION

Using Symbols and Abbreviations 2

Here are some additional tips to save writing time when you take notes.

Use as few vowels as possible

bewildering	bewldrng
ceremony	cermny
cremated	cremtd
reassured	reassrd

Use these abbreviations

someone	s/o
something	s/t
with	w/
without	w/o

Omit the final letters of the word

elaborate	elab
reception	recep
significance	signif

Use other conventional symbols

→	causes, leads to
←	is the result of

🔊
CD 2, TR 15

A **Listen to the sentences. As you listen, write the sentences in notetaking form below. Use symbols and abbreviations. Then use your notes to read the sentences to a classmate.**

1. _____

2. _____

3. _____

4. _____

B **Discourse Cues** **Number the following excerpts from the lecture from 1 to 5 in the order that you think you will probably hear them. Discuss with a partner or as a class the discourse cues that helped you figure out the order.**

_____ After the baby is born, most families participate in some kind of spiritual ceremony...

_____ Today I want to talk about customs in the United States, not all customs of course, but customs surrounding certain important events in almost everyone's life.

_____ The last passage I'm going to talk about today is the passage from life to death.

_____ As I said before, in a society so large and diverse as the United States, customs can vary greatly.

_____ Today let's look at some widely accepted customs and traditions of most Americans concerning three of life's most important events, or passages: birth, marriage, and death.

🔊
CD 2, TR 16
FIRST LISTENING

Listen to the lecture and take notes. Look at the lecturer's visual aids as you listen. These may help you understand parts of the lecture.

Introduction

> **Customs and Traditions**
>
> Introduction
> Birth
> Marriage
> Death

Subtopic 1: _____

> **Birth**
>
> • Baby shower before
> • Spiritual ceremony after

Subtopic 2: _____

> **Marriage**
>
> • Engagement
> • Shower
> • Wedding ceremony

Subtopic 3: _____

Death

- The deceased
- Funeral service / religious ceremony
- Memorial service

CD 2, TR 17

SECOND LISTENING

Listen to the lecture again and make your notes as complete as possible.

THIRD LISTENING

CD 2, TR 18

A You will hear part of the lecture again. Listen and complete the notes by adding the information from the box.

| cermny | fath's | ppl | @ | = | w/ | 100s |

Marr. ++custm & tradi, esp for weddg
- Not nec for man to ask _____ permiss.
  - mst yng _____ want parnts' approv
- Tradi _____ man gives diamnd engagmnt ring
- Weddng
  - Bride's fam pays
  - _____
    - simple _____ few frnds & fam OR
    - elabrt w/ _____ of ppl
  - Recept. follows ceremony
    - simple: cookies OR
    - elab: dinnr _____ hotl w/mus & dancng

B Compare your answers with a partner. Then compare the notes in **A** with the notes you took for this part of the lecture.

ACCURACY CHECK

CD 2, TR 19

A Listen to the following questions, and write short answers. Use your notes. You will hear each question one time only.

1. _____
2. _____
3. _____
4. _____
5. _____
6. _____
7. _____
8. _____
9. _____
10. _____

B Check your answers with your teacher. If your score is less than 70 percent, you may need to listen to the lecture again and rewrite some of your notes.

ORAL SUMMARY

Use your notes to create an oral summary of the lecture with your partner. As you work together, add details to your notes that your partner included but you had missed.

DISCUSSION

Discuss the following statements with a classmate or in a small group.

1. Is it surprising that people in the United States, with its great racial and ethnic diversity, celebrate birth, marriage, and death in similar ways? Why?

2. Death is a topic that is very difficult for most Americans to talk about. What reasons might there be for this?

3. It is considered bad luck for the groom to see the bride in her wedding dress before the ceremony. What might be a reason for this superstition? Does your culture have superstitions connected to weddings?

PRE-READING

The following Reading is about traditional marriage customs in parts of rural Africa. Before you read, answer the following questions. Share your answers with a classmate.

1. Which of the marriage customs described in the lecture would be most likely to exist in a variety of other countries, including traditional rural cultures in Africa?

2. What is a ritual? Describe one marriage ritual that is widely practiced in your culture.

READING

Now read the article.

African Marriage Rituals

Morocco—Berber

In Morocco's High Atlas mountains, a young woman may catch the eye of an admirer at the yearly bride's fair in the village of Imilchil. If the young woman's parents' approve, a courtship begins. This is the period of time during which the couple and their families develop a relationship, in preparation for marriage. For widows and divorced women, the Imilchil fair is an open market, with marriages performed right then and there.

Before a young bride's wedding, her mother rubs her legs with henna, a flowering plant that is used to dye the skin a reddish brown color. This is a ritual that her people believe keeps evil spirits away. On the wedding day, the mother says a bittersweet good-bye to her daughter by kissing her knee. After the wedding ceremony, the young bride travels by mule to her new husband's home. Once there, one of his female relatives will lift her off the mule so that her feet don't touch the ground and risk evil spirits entering her body.

Days of parties followed by nights of singing and dancing come next for the bride, who has captured the liver—the Berber symbol of love—of the man who has promised to protect her.

Ethiopia—Karo

The beauty of Ethiopia's Orno River Valley is matched by its people, who decorate their bodies to improve their physical appearance. The 500 or so Karo have very few possessions, so they rely on nature and trade for decoration. When a Karo girl reaches puberty, razorlike cuts are made in the skin of her stomach. Ashes are then rubbed into the cuts to make them heal in a raised pattern. This, Karo men told us, increases her beauty.

Karo women also apply face paint to attract a mate, often copying the colors and patterns that are found on local birds' feathers. In addition, they wear necklaces made of banana seeds that they have collected, or glass beads that they get from trading at small markets a three-days' walk away from their homes.

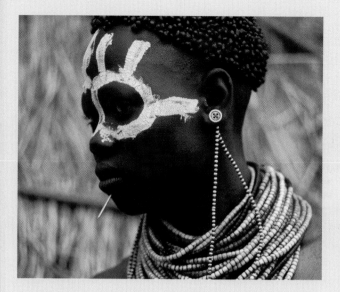

paid over time, in the form of both money and live animals, particularly cattle.

A two-week separation of the bride from her family marks the second stage, when other women teach her how to be a good Ndebele wife. When this period of separation ends, the Ndebele bride emerges wearing colorful beaded hoops around her waist and legs. These imitate the female form that the Ndebele so greatly admire. The Ndebele bride is also given a marriage blanket, which she will wear to special events for the rest of her life.

The third stage of Ndebele marriage is completed only after the woman has given birth to her first child. Up until then, she is not considered truly married.

When the summer has passed and the harvest is complete, courtship season begins. Unmarried Karo youth, decorated with face paint, beaded necklaces, and many bracelets, join in joyful dances. A man signals his interest to a woman during the singing and dancing. For many the excitement will lead to engagement, marriage, and a lifetime together.

South Africa—Ndebele

Ndebele weddings are celebrated in three stages, which can take years to conclude. They begin with the negotiation of *lobola*, or bride price, which is

DISCUSSION

Discuss these questions with a classmate.

1. What similarities can you see between marriage customs in the United States and in parts of rural Africa—courtship and engagement, the marriage ceremony, gift giving, and so on?

2. Of the three cultures mentioned in the reading, which one has marriage customs that are most different from those in the United States? Explain.

3. Which of the marriage customs mentioned in the lecture and the reading were the most interesting or surprising to you?

PURSUING THE TOPIC

Explore the topic of this chapter further by doing the following.

Watch the movie *The Father of the Bride*, a 1991 comedy about a father whose beloved daughter is about to be married. Be prepared to discuss the movie with your classmates.

Through the Eyes of a Critic

High-fiving iguana on the Galápagos Islands, Ecuador

BEFORE VIEWING

TOPIC PREVIEW

Who is an artist's most honest critic? Rank the following people from 1 to 5
(*5* = the best or most honest critic and *1* = the worst or least honest critic).
Discuss your order with a partner.

_____ a. the artist's mother or father

_____ b. the artist's husband or wife

_____ c. the artist's young son or daughter

_____ d. a stranger

_____ e. an art expert or specialist

VOCABULARY PREVIEW

A Read the definitions of these key words and phrases that you will hear during
the video.

missing out on not able to enjoy something because of other responsibilities

hugged put one's arms around someone

never mind that don't worry about that; forget that

the surface the top or outside part of something that you can see or touch

curious wanting to learn more about someone or something

illuminating shining light on something

took me ages took me a very long time

idiot a stupid or foolish person

a high five a gesture where two people slap each other's hand above their heads in a
show of greeting, pleasure, or victory

B Work with a partner and write vocabulary from **A** in the blanks in the sentences.

1. It _____ to complete my research paper. I stayed up all night!

2. I know my son thinks I'm a(n) _____ whenever I ask him a question about my cell phone.

3. It helps for a photojournalist to be _____.

4. If you don't go to the club, you'll be _____ a good time.

5. After the blackout, people started _____ their homes with candles.

6. We won the game and everyone in the room gave each other _____.

7. Janet cried when she broke her father's favorite sunglasses. But he just _____ her and said, "_____."

8. Whales come to _____ of the ocean to breathe.

VIEWING

🖵 FIRST VIEWING

Watch the video, and then compare your first impressions with a partner. Talk about what you remember, what surprised you, and what interested you.

🖵 SECOND VIEWING

Watch the video again. Listen for the missing words and write them in the blanks.

1. And then I felt a little bit _____ for myself. It's like I'm _____ so much.

2. So I was sitting down with a _____ showing him this land iguana with this Galapagos mockingbird, talking about this very interesting sort of collaborative _____.

3. It's a nice symbiotic _____. And he was like _____ by this.

4. And when there's a big predator, they will get very _____. And they will hover. And the big orca will _____ up perhaps.

5. This is a _____ iguana. And, yeah, I was sneaking up to it.

⬛ THIRD VIEWING

Complete these notes as you watch the video. Write only important words, not full sentences, and abbreviate common words.

MK: Comes home from Galap trip
A: Dad, You're home! How was _____?
MK: _____
A: Any gd pics?
MK: Yeah
A: _____
MK: Shows pic of mkingbd on top of liz
A: Fascinat'd
MK: Shows pic of sea lions and birds over orcas
A: _____
MK: Shows last set of pics
A: Best _____
MK: Why?
A: _____

AFTER VIEWING

ORAL SUMMARY

Use your notes to create an oral summary of the video with your partner. As you work together, add details to your notes that your partner included but you had missed.

DISCUSSION

Discuss the following questions with a classmate or in a small group.

1. Why do you think Mattias Klum came home "feeling sorry" for himself?

2. What reaction do you think the father expected when Anskar first walked into the kitchen and saw his Dad? What was Anskar interested in instead?

3. Why did the audience find the son's questions and comments so funny?

4. What does the title of the video mean?

Challenges at Home and Abroad

Earth's city lights (NASA)

Multiculturalism

assimilate → get used to.

hearding

TOPIC PREVIEW

Answer the following questions with a partner or your classmates.

تجمع
في الحياة بس

1. What happens to metals like iron and chromium put together inside a melting pot to melt?

alloy.

2. Why do you think the melting pot and the patchwork quilt are often used as metaphors, or symbols, of the multicultural character of U.S. society?

explanations

3. Does cultural diversity in a society bring more benefits or more problems?

A multicultural parade moves through Little Italy and Chinatown in New York City.

VOCABULARY PREVIEW

A Read through the sentences below, which are missing vocabulary from the lecture. As you read, try to imagine which words would fit in the blanks. Then listen to the sentences and write the missing words in the blanks.

CD 3, TR 1

1. A melting pot is the traditional _metaphor_ for the way different groups of immigrants came together in the United States.

2. In theory, the result of many nationalities _blending_ together is one big, _homogeneous_, culture.

3. It is like an _alloy_, a combination of all the different parts mixed together into a single whole that is different from each of its parts.

4. Many groups, especially African, Asian, and American Indian, have at times been _excluded_ from participating fully in society through _segregation_ and discrimination.

5. U.S. society does not _assimilate_ a new cultural group until later, after the new immigrants are viewed with less prejudice.

6. The metaphor of the patchwork quilt seems right to the multiculturalists because they see the United States as a _mosaic_ of separate subcultures, each one distinct from the others.

7. Of the 1.6 million children in the United States who are _adopted_, about 18 percent are of a different race than their adopting parents, making their families _multiracial_.

8. Cultural influences have distinct sources. We _inherit_ some of our culture from our families. We _absorb_ some of our culture subconsciously from just living in the culture—through TV and videos.

9. With _assimilation_, individuals become part of the larger culture by accepting much, if not all, of that culture.

10. The pluralistic view differs from the single culture view in that it does not mean that immigrants must forget or _deny_ their original culture.

B Check the spelling of the vocabulary words with your teacher. Discuss the meanings of these words and any other unfamiliar words in the sentences.

PREDICTIONS

Think about the questions in the Topic Preview on page 64 and the sentences you heard in the Vocabulary Preview. Write three questions that you think will be answered in the lecture. Share your questions with your classmates.

con → aginst
pro → for

NOTETAKING PREPARATION

Transition Words and Phrases

Formal speech, like formal writing, is characterized by more frequent use of transition words and phrases. Transition words like such as *however, therefore*, and *in fact* help a listener understand the relationship between ideas and sentences in the lecture.

A good understanding of transition words will make a formal lecture easier to follow.

On the other hand and *however* point out contrasts between two ideas.
For instance and *for example* present examples.
In fact is used for emphasis.
Rather is used like *instead* to signal an alternative.
Furthermore is used like *also* to signal an additional point.
Therefore and *consequently* mean *for this reason* to signal a result or consequence.

A Read through the sentences below. Choose the best transition word from the box above to complete each sentence. Write the transition word in the blank.

1. The melting pot metaphor is a very old one. __In falt__, it's been used since the nineteenth century.

2. Culture comes to people in different ways. __For Instance__, we inherit some, and we absorb some.

3. There are many proponents of the multiculturalist view; __However__, I don't really agree with this view.

4. The multiculturalists don't use the metaphor of the melting pot. __Rather__, they use the patchwork quilt.

5. Some existing groups were excluded from participating fully in society; __an addition al__ newly arrived groups were discriminated against.

6. We are not satisfied with the metaphors for U.S. culture in this lecture. __therefore__, we are going to look for a new one.

B **Discourse Cues** Number the following excerpts from the lecture from 1 to 5 in the order that you think you will probably hear them. Discuss with a partner or as a class the discourse cues that helped you figure out the order.

__2__ So, first is the single culture view of the United States as a "melting pot."

__4__ This last cultural view, the pluralistic view, is a combination of the first two.

__5__ To conclude, the United States has always reflected the cultures of its immigrants.

__1__ Let me begin today's lecture by explaining the meaning of the word culture.

__3__ Now let's move on to another view of U.S. culture.

FIRST LISTENING

(CD 3, TR 2)

A Listen to the beginning of the lecture. Circle the set of notes below that best records the information you hear.

a.
```
Cultr = trad + shared belfs & val
     Ex. in fam; ed; bus.; pol; ent.
US cultr ?? ppl othr countries & Am's
Contrst 3 ways US cult seen
   • Sing cult (old)
   • Multicult. (new)
   • Pluralistic
```

b.
```
Cultr ≠ traditions; = blfs + val
     EX: fam. struc, ed. sys, etc.
Ppl fr othr cultrs, ? Am cultr
Nature US cult ? — contrast 3
   disc ↑ yrs
   decide = logical
   old (sing.), new (multi), third (pl)
```

(CD 3, TR 3)

B Now listen to the whole lecture and take notes. Look at the lecturer's visual aids as you listen. These may help you understand parts of the lecture.

Subtopic 1: Single Culture

(handwritten) the tradinal in diff cult.

comprized,

many groups   excluded

sagregoltion

enterpioralton   Italian & ireish

us solity

2 or 3 gentation

Single Culture View

U.S. = Melting pot
    Homogeneous culture
Myth?
    Excluded groups

Subtopic 2: Multicultural

(handwritten) atthik

the naetahave and revital

they see as amsices

us cult, little no meksing

Intemarrid, to Indedicate

then. 1- with, black.   very few the lack

1.6 were adopted.   or abrood   of exseption morphan,

Multiculturalist View

U.S. = a patchwork quilt (6)
    Many different subcultures
Opposition
    Ethnic and racial mixing

we do max some.

say,

Subtopic 3: _Pluralist_

'share with others
from family
from ~~TV~~ TV or gams.
// many colture

Inde

recniz the emeltion

U.s. Refcteteb contina

immegrent.

is tollareat other people

Pluralistic View
Combination of 1 & 2
Cultural influences
Inheritance
Absorption
Choice
Role of assimilation

→ g

SECOND LISTENING

CD 3, TR 4

Listen to the lecture again and make your notes as complete as possible.

THIRD LISTENING

CD 3, TR 5

A You will hear part of the lecture again. Listen and complete the notes by adding the information from the box.

i.e.   M.P.   →   cult   B.   =   diff

1. Singl. __cult__ view = U.S. as Melting Pot
   A. __M.P.__ = trad. metaph
      M.P. ← mix of __diff__ gps immigs blending
      __→__ big homog. cult
      __i.e.__ comb of diff parts = new whole
      __B__ Many think one cult __=__ myth

B Compare your answers with a partner. Then compare the notes in **A** with the notes you took for this part of the lecture.

ACCURACY CHECK

CD 3, TR 6

A Listen to the questions, and write short answers. Use your notes. You will hear each question one time only.

Handwritten margin notes (left side):
- what is cult?
- 2 groups diff?
- oldest cult?
- matphore?
- ing — myth £ of 3 groups or w. x.
- % of marrige
- adopted from?
- 3 views of pluralistic
- what generation

Handwritten answers:
1. trad + shared belefs & val
2. American & other countries.
3. single cultu
4. melting pot
5. AF. Asia. Am Indian
6. apatch work quilt or the mosic
7. 15%
8. Asia / latin America
9. Inheritance, Absorption and choice
10. second & third generation.

B Check your answers with your teacher. If your score is less than 70 percent, you may need to listen to the lecture again and rewrite some of your notes.

ORAL SUMMARY

Use your notes to create an oral summary of the lecture with a partner. As you work together, add details to your notes that your partner included but you had missed.

DISCUSSION

Discuss the following questions with a classmate or in a small group.

1. Which of the three views of U.S. culture makes the most sense to you? Explain.

2. How important is it for immigrants to assimilate to the culture in a new country?

3. How open is your country of origin to influences from other cultures? Do people who spend long periods of time there assimilate to the culture, or do they maintain their own cultures?

4. Can you think of a particular metaphor that fits your culture?

PRE-READING

The following Reading is about the city of Marseille in France. Before you read, answer the following questions. Share your answers with a classmate.

1. What does the title of the article suggest to you about the population of the city of Marseille?

2. Marseille is on the sea, in the southern part of France. Where do you think immigrants to Marseille come from?

READING

Now read the article.

Marseille's Melting Pot

As more European countries become nations of immigrants, the city of Marseille in southern France may be a vision of the future, even a model of multiculturalism. In November 2005, with riots happening in just about every other French city's immigrant-filled housing projects, Marseille stayed cool.

Some local people believe that the Marseille miracle of social peace has a lot to do with its beaches, which serve as its great melting pot. Farouk Youssoufa, 25, met his 20-year-old wife, Mina, at one of Marseille's beaches. Youssoufa was born on a French island in the Comoros between Tanzania and Madagascar, and his skin is as black as anyone's in Africa. Mina is the fair-skinned French-born daughter of Algerian immigrants. "The new generation is much more of a mixture," says Youssoufa, who works with boys and girls of almost every skin tone and ethnic background at a cultural center in Marseille. On the beach, especially, "there are a lot of different communities that mix," Youssoufa says one hot afternoon in May. "Voilà: With time we've learned to live together."

Jean-Claude Gaudin, the mayor of Marseille, points out that the beach isn't the only geographic feature that has kept the city's melting pot bubbling. "Marseille's good luck is that it is surrounded by a belt of mountains." Immigrants and long-time residents have learned to live more or less on top of each other. When the country's growing economy needed foreign workers for factories, many French cities built housing projects for immigrants in distant suburbs.

"We did the opposite," says Gaudin. "We built in the city. Marseille is the oldest city in France. It's been in existence for 2,600 years. It's a port, and so we have always been used to having foreigners come here. The city itself is composed," he says, "of populations from abroad who came because of international developments." After 1915, Armenians began arriving. In the 1930s Italians who fled fascism settled in Marseille. And in 1962, after France had given up control of Algeria, Morocco, and Tunisia, tens of thousands of *pieds-noirs*, or "black feet," flooded Marseille. They were actually white French citizens fleeing newly independent Algeria, where many had lived for generations.

At the same time, Gaudin explains, Marseille gradually filled with other people—*issus de l'immigration*—produced by immigration. "That means that often the grandparents were in Algeria, the parents came here, and the grandchildren are French but have an Arab last name," says Gaudin. In other words, people who are French by birth but are still viewed as "foreigners."

Yet the mayor of Marseille can only guess how many of his city's residents are *issus de l'immigration*. He does not know how many are of Arab or African

The beach at Marseille where people of all ethnicities mix and mingle

descent. He does not know how many have Muslim roots. In France, it's against the law for any government official to record a citizen's race, religion, or ethnicity. Church and state are not only separate, but religion is officially ignored. If you are French, you are French: nothing more, nothing less, and nothing else.

Yet Gaudin knows that even for the second and third generations, assimilation does not always come easily. The challenge for any city with a large immigrant population is rarely how to deal with the first wave of arrivals, but how their children and grandchildren will adapt, or not.

DISCUSSION

Discuss these questions with a classmate.

1. Based on what you learned from the lecture, which of the three ways of looking at culture—the single culture view, the multiculturalist view, or the pluralistic view—best describes the situation in Marseille?

2. In what ways do you think the French attitude toward cultural assimilation is different from the American attitude?

3. What are the differences between how the French government and the U.S. government deal with immigration?

PURSUING THE TOPIC

Explore the topic of this chapter further by doing the following.

Watch the movie *Green Card*, a 1990s romantic comedy about a French man who marries an American woman in order to be able to obtain a visa to stay in the United States. Or watch the movie *My Big Fat Greek Wedding*, a 2002 family comedy about maintaining Greek culture and tradition in modern-day America. Be prepared to discuss the movie with your classmates.

[handwritten notes: blue-collar → service plumber factory. white-collar → educated business. demestic violent: when the man hert women ♀ vs ♂ uncommon.]

TOPIC PREVIEW

Answer the following questions with a partner or your classmates.

1. Do you think there has been an increase in violent crime in recent years? Why or why not?

2. What is the difference between "blue-collar" and "white-collar" crime?

3. Which of the following do you think is more responsible for whether a young person turns to crime—their family, their school, or the criminal justice system?

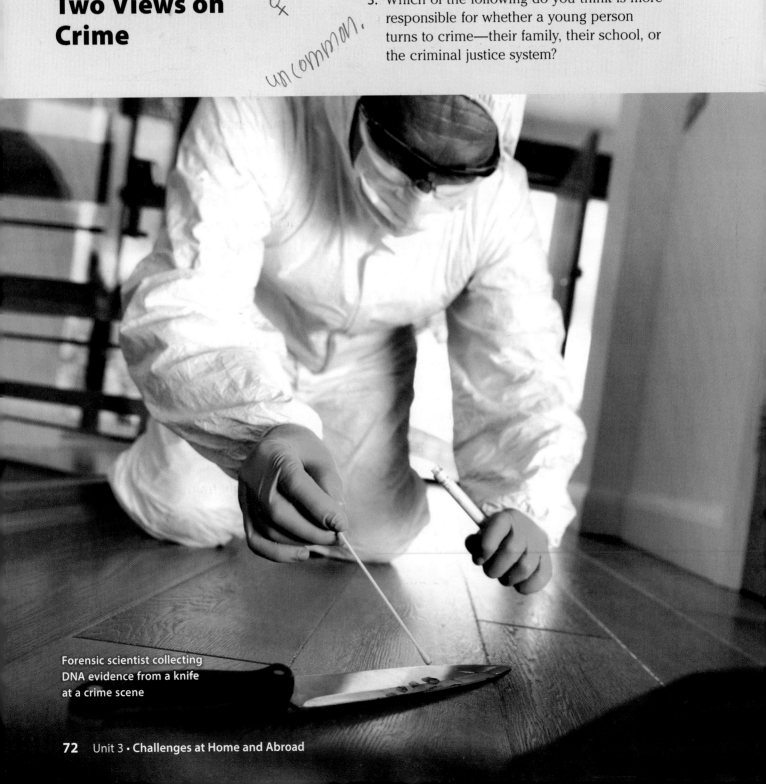

Forensic scientist collecting DNA evidence from a knife at a crime scene

VOCABULARY PREVIEW

CD 3, TR 7

A Read through the sentences below, which are missing vocabulary from the lecture. As you read, try to imagine which words would fit in the blanks. Then listen to the sentences and write the missing words in the blanks.

1. Some experts _attribute_ this drop in the crime rate to _demographics_: the U.S. population is getting older, and older people commit fewer crimes.

2. In recent years there has been stricter law _enforcement_ in big cities, and very tough _penalties_ have been imposed on repeat offenders in general.

3. The encouraging statistics for violent crime may not be true for white-collar crime, crimes that include _bribery_, political corruption, _embezzlement_, and corporate policies that endanger workers and the public.

4. So, some people _blame_ criminal behavior on society's _shortcomings_, or failures.

5. There are root causes like racism, poverty, and _injustice_.

6. In this theory, people become _alienated_ from society because they do not have many of the benefits that most Americans have.

7. The _underclass_ is that part of the population that typically fits the following profile: poor, unemployed, badly educated, nonwhite, and living in older city neighborhoods.

8. According to this theory, society tries to _deter_ this aggressiveness and potential violence in two ways: by socializing us and, if that fails, by punishing us.

9. Society _socialized_ us by giving us values—values to prevent killing and stealing, for example. And society also gives us values for honesty, _compassion_, and kindness.

10. Our _conscience_ functions as a deterrent to violence and criminal behavior because we have been taught right from wrong.

B Check the spelling of the vocabulary words with your teacher. Discuss the meanings of these words and any other unfamiliar words in the sentences.

PREDICTIONS

Think about the questions in the Topic Preview on page 72 and the sentences you heard in the Vocabulary Preview. Write three questions that you think will be answered in the lecture. Share your questions with your classmates.

NOTETAKING PREPARATION

Using Indentation to Organize Notes 2

In chapter 5, you learned to organize your notes visually with indents and bullets. Ideas and information you hear can have more than two levels of importance. These less important details, examples, and ideas can be further indented to the right. A symbol, such as a hyphen (–) or a plus sign (+), can be used to indicate these other levels.

For example, information about solutions to crime in a part of this lecture could be organized like this:

Possible solutions to crime
- the family's role
  - socializing the children
    + children respect themselves and others

A Read the phrases below and decide their order of importance. Then complete the note outline by adding the phrases. Show order of importance with indenting and symbols.

~~help them feel like part of society~~ / good education / good health care / overcome the alienation of the underclass / ~~society's role~~ / give them the same benefits that others have / ~~employment~~

society's role
  Give some benefits, overcome alienation./help them feel
    - help them feel like part of society

    + employment

B **Discourse Cues** Number the following excerpts from the lecture from 1 to 5 in the order that you think you will probably hear them. Discuss with a partner or as a class the discourse cues that helped you figure out the order.

_3_ Well, let's go on and take a closer look at both theories.

_1_ Today we're going to look at American attitudes about human nature and crime.

_4_ OK, to start off with, people who believe social problems are caused by unequal opportunities prefer the first theory: that people are good by nature.

_2_ Today I'd like to take a look at two different theories.

_5_ Now, to go back to something I talked about earlier. This second theory helps us understand white-collar crime, I think.

FIRST LISTENING

CD 3, TR 8

A Listen to the beginning of the lecture. Circle the set of notes below that best records the information you hear.

a.

> Am att to hum ntr & crime
>   CR 13.4% 2010
>   CR ↓ old ppl < yng ppl
>   Law enfrmnt & penalts ↑
>   Wh-collar cr ↑
>   • pub not afrd
>   • incld disc. of cr in US
>   Theor of cr = belief, hum ntr
>   • ppl good
>   • ppl aggress & violent
>   Solutns to cr in US

b.

> Am attitudes abt human nature & crime
>   • stats
>   – FBI: v. cr. ↓ 13.4% 2001–10 (ex: ag,
>   aslt, rob, murd, etc.)
>   + US pop older / older= ↓ cr,
>   + ↑ enfrcmnt & >penalts rep. cr
>   – Wht coll. C ↑ or ↓ ? (stats hard to
>   get) (ex: brib, pol corrup, embez., dang.
>   corp pol's)
>   • 2 theor C bsd on hum ntr — look at
>   – Theory 1: ppl good
>   – Theory 2 ppl aggress, so can be v.
>   – Pos. solutions to C in US

CD 3, TR 9

B Now listen to the whole lecture and take notes. Look at the lecturer's visual aids as you listen. These may help you understand parts of the lecture.

Subtopic 1: ___good___

> FBI : v. cr 13.4
> – wht-coll. cr or ↓. somezism.
> parents. ox.(brib. polcorrupebez.
> –pos. solutions to C in US.

> Environment → Criminal behavior
> • Root causes in U.S. society
> • Existence of an underclass

Subtopic 2: _____

> ss.det. [socizel
>   puneshement.
> values, e.g. Killing

> Aggressive nature → Violent behavior
> • Socialization
> • Punishment
> • Connection to white-collar crime

Subtopic 3: _____

gov. — over come, underclass.
Help ppl.

Meeting the Challenge
- Role of family
- Role of government

CD 3, TR 10

SECOND LISTENING

Listen to the lecture again and make your notes as complete as possible.

THIRD LISTENING

CD 3, TR 11

A You will hear part of the lecture again. Listen and complete the notes by adding the information from the box.

| BUT | ex | NO | polit. | SO | → | wh-coll |

Theor #2 explains _____ C
- *wh-collar crim. not usully under-class*
  - *busnssmn*
  - *_____*
  - *bankrs*
- *have benef's of soc., _____ good ed, good neigh.*
- *_____ for ? reason*
  - *_____ well-dev. conscience*
  - *_____ ntrl aggress*
    + *_____ C*

B Compare your answers with a partner. Then compare the notes in **A** with the notes you took for this part of the lecture.

education

AFTER LISTENING

ACCURACY CHECK

🔊 CD 3, TR 12

A Listen to the following questions and write short answers. Use your notes. You will hear each question one time only.

B/c they don't have the binifits or what the rom have.

violent aggreseve ←

sholized paseshement →

1. ? % Cri ↓ 2001-2010. / 13.4 %
2. 3 e.x. of whitecoller Crim. / bribry, embez, pol corrup
3. ? 3 short coming → crim. / racism, poverty, Injustice.
4. why some criminal alianited from socaity.
5. poor ppl, bad edu. → Crim. / No
6. How 2nd theary see people? aggresuve by nature.
7. 2nd theary detor in 2 ways?
8. How white color crime diff? They are not part of underclass.
9. 3 thing society provide for underclass? edu, Health care, employment.
10. determing crime Punishment, first or 2nd thearg?

goes with second thearey. ←

B Check your answers with your teacher. If your score is less than 70 percent, you may need to listen to the lecture again and rewrite some of your notes.

ORAL SUMMARY

Use your notes to create an oral summary of the lecture with your partner. As you work together, add details to your notes that your partner included but you had missed.

DISCUSSION

Discuss the following questions with a classmate or in a small group.

1. Which type of crime, violent crime or white-collar crime, causes the most damage to society? Explain.

2. Have you seen examples of how racism and poverty can lead people to crime?

3. Which do you think is more effective in keeping most people from committing crime: a strong conscience or a fear of punishment?

4. Should governments spend more money on keeping criminals in prison or on improving public education?

PRE-READING

The following Reading is about the nation of Singapore. Before you read, answer the following questions. Share your answers with a classmate.

1. What do you know about Singapore? For example, where is it located? Is it a rich or a poor country? What kind of government does it have? Is there any crime?

2. Look at the title of the article. The word *solution* implies that there is or was a problem. What do you think the problem could be?

READING

Now read the article.

The Singapore Solution

Singapore is often called the Switzerland of Southeast Asia. The tiny island gained independence from Britain in 1963 and, in one generation, transformed itself into a country where the income for its 3.7 million citizens is larger than in many European countries. Singapore also has excellent education and health systems and almost no government corruption, 90 percent of people own their own homes, and you never see homeless people.

Achieving all this has involved a delicate balance between what some Singaporeans refer to as "the big stick and the big carrot." First of all, the carrot: rapid financial growth. And the stick? Strict government control of citizens' lives. Racial and religious disharmony? They're simply not allowed, and no one steals anyone else's wallet.

The Singapore Flyer, the world's tallest Ferris wheel

Behind the "Singapore Model," a unique mix of economic empowerment and tightly controlled personal liberties, is Lee Kuan Yew. From a wealthy Chinese family, Cambridge University graduate Lee was Singapore's first prime minister, serving for 26 years and then as senior minister for another 15. His current title of minister mentor (MM) was established when his son, Lee Hsien Loong, became prime minister in 2004.

In creating the "Singapore Model," the MM turned a tiny country with no natural resources and a mix of ethnic groups into "Singapore, Inc." He attracted foreign investment, made English the official language, created a superefficient government, and eliminated corruption.

To lead a society, the MM says "one must understand human nature." He says, "The Confucian theory was man could be improved, but I'm not sure he can be. He can be trained, he can be disciplined." In Singapore that has meant lots of rules (no gum chewing and spitting on sidewalks) with fines and occasional notices in the newspaper about those who break the rules. Following the rules becomes automatic; you don't see very many police in Singapore. As one resident says, "The cop is inside our heads."

Singapore, maybe more than anywhere else, raises a basic question: Are financial success and personal security worth the extreme limits placed on individual freedom?

The Singapore government is aware that there are problems with its highly controlled society. One concern is the "creativity crisis." This is the fear that Singapore's schools, with their traditional educational methods, do not produce original thinkers. Another concern is a direct result of Singapore's overly successful population-control program, started in the 1970s. Today Singaporeans are simply not having enough children, so immigrants are needed to keep the population growing.

But there is a positive side. You could feel it during the "We Are the World" performance in the National Day show. On stage were representatives of Singapore's major ethnic groups: the Chinese, Malays, and Indians. After violent protests in the 1960s, the government started a strict system in public housing that required the different ethnic groups to live together. The purpose of this system may have been to control the population, but the apparently sincere expression of racial harmony at the performance was impressive.

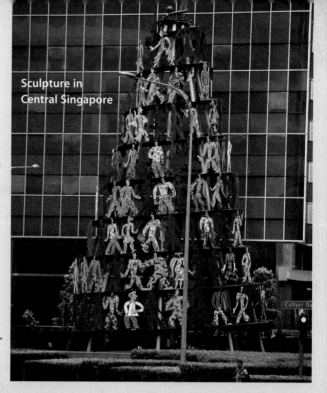

Sculpture in Central Singapore

There is something called Singaporean, and it is real. Whatever people's complaints, Singapore is their home, and they love it despite everything. It makes you like the place, too.

DISCUSSION

Discuss these questions with a classmate.

1. Do any of the reasons mentioned in the lecture for a recent drop in crime in the United States also apply to Singapore? Which reasons? Explain your answer.

2. Which of the two theories of crime discussed in the lecture would Lee Kuan Yew of Singapore be most likely to agree with? Explain your answer using information in the reading and in the lecture.

3. Would the ways in which the Singaporean government has addressed social problems such as crime work in the United States? Why or why not? Use examples from the lecture to support your opinion.

PURSUING THE TOPIC

Explore the topic of this chapter further by doing the following.

The Web site for the Federal Bureau of Investigation (FBI) has a large amount of information about all aspects of crime in the United States. Individually or with a partner, choose a topic that interests you and read about it. Write up the details for a short presentation to the class.

www.fbi.gov

CHAPTER 9

Threat

Sanctions

The United States and the World

TOPIC PREVIEW

Discuss the following questions with a partner or your classmates.

1. Ten years from now, which country, or countries, do you think will be the most powerful in the world?

2. What kinds of responsibilities, if any, do powerful countries have to other countries?

3. Rank these three kinds of power in order from most to least important: (a) military, (b) economic, (c) political. Explain your reasons.

Coke bottle design contest held In Nanjing, China

VOCABULARY PREVIEW

CD 3, TR 13

A Read through the sentences below, which are missing vocabulary from the lecture. As you read, try to imagine which words would fit in the blanks. Then listen to the sentences and write the missing words in the blanks.

1. Some experts are __Predict__ that China will become the new global leader because of its size as well as its economic and military strength.

2. It seems very likely that the United States will remain very important globally, at least for the __Foreseeable__ future.

3. The United States can also help maintain financial __stability__ in the world because of the size of its economy.

4. I'm describing hard power—that is, the __thrait__ or use of force.

5. This force can be economic, which would include __sanetions__ against trading with a country.

6. For better or for worse, the United States has taken on the role of keeping a certain __balance__ of power in many parts of the world.

7. The United States is also a member of NATO, an organization of mostly European nations __devoted__ to keeping peace in the world.

8. ASEAN countries like Indonesia and Malaysia engage in massive trade with China and may at times feel a little __intimidate__ by China's size and power.

9. Soft power does not come from economic or military threat, but from how attractive or __persuasive__ a country's culture, political ideals, and policies are.

10. The United States is still a __magnet__ to immigrants for both political and economic reasons.

11. My goal today was to give you a __framework__ for understanding some of what you learn in the media about the U.S. economic, military, and political influence in the world today.

B Check the spelling of the vocabulary words with your teacher. Discuss the meanings of these words and any other unfamiliar words in the sentences.

PREDICTIONS

Think about the questions in the Topic Preview on page 80 and the sentences you heard in the Vocabulary Preview. Write three questions that you think will be answered in the lecture. Share your questions with your classmates.

HUSSEIN

Nothing can stop me. I'm all the way UP.↑

NOTETAKING PREPARATION

Acronyms and Abbreviations 1

Acronyms are formed from the first letter of each word in a group or name. They are pronounced as words. For example, BRIC, which stands for Brazil, Russia, India, and China, is pronounced /brɪk/.

Abbreviations, like UN (United Nations), are different from acronyms and are pronounced letter by letter. Two common abbreviations usually used only in written language come from Latin: e.g., used for "for example," and i.e., used for "that is."

A Practice saying these acronyms and abbreviations with a partner.

Impo.

1. NATO (North Atlantic Treaty Organization /ˈneɪ.toʊ/)
2. ASEAN (Association of Southeast Asian Nations /əˈziː.ən/),
3. UNESCO (United Nations Educational, Social, and Cultural Organization /juːˈnes.koʊ/)
4. EU (European Union)

B Listen and complete the following sentences using acronyms and abbreviations.

CD 3, TR 14

1. Many countries have better economies, __e.x.__, __BRIC__.
2. __UNESCO__ is an important arm of the _____.
3. France is a member of __NATO__.
4. Some __ASEAN__ countries are small, __e.g.__, Cambodia.
5. Some people think the __EU__ countries should become a federation, __i.e.__, have a political structure that is similar to the __USA__.

C Discourse Cues Number the following excerpts from the lecture from 1 to 5 in the order that you think you will probably hear them. Discuss with a partner or as a class the discourse cues that helped you figure out the order.

No! coz No Time!

__3__ First, let me give you some of the economic reasons Yetiv gives for why the United States will probably continue to be an important player globally.

__4__ Now let's move on to the United States' use of what I'm describing today as hard power—that is, the threat or use of force.

__2__ Professor Steve Yetiv of Old Dominion University in Virginia wrote three articles in which he gave a number of reasons why believes the United States will remain a global leader.

__1__ Today I'd like to discuss the role of the United States in the world.

__5__ Soft power does not come from economic or military threat, but from how attractive or persuasive a country's culture, political ideals, and policies are.

FIRST LISTENING

CD 3, TR 15

Listen to the lecture and take notes. Look at the lecturer's visual aids as you listen. These may help you understand parts of the lecture.

Introduction

past ← hos been groth.

now ← china & USA
military & economic
USA remin globly.

The U.S. and the World
- Introduction
- The U.S. economy
- U.S. hard power
- U.S. soft power

3 cotagories.

Subtopic 1: economic

Am.   It has money. or earth

help findchel b/c of the ecomic
political
siz e ecomimy
Huge market other contries

global currency.
less attractiv = yewan → chinas carreng

Economic Reasons
- Ability to help others in crisis
- Ability to maintain financial stability
- U.S. dollar = global currency

Subtopic 2: hard power

ekonmic

us, will help in many punt of
the world

Hard Power
- Middle East
- NATO
- ASEAN

Involved the Asion

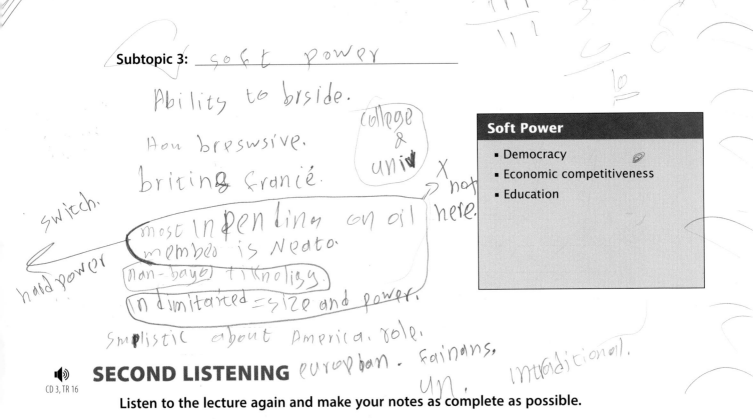

Subtopic 3: _Soft power_

Ability to brside.

Hou breswsive.

briting Franié.

switch.

most Inpenling on oil
membed is Neato.

nan-baye tiknoligy.

In dimitarted = size and power.

Smplistic about America. role.

hard power

college & univ

x hot here.

Soft Power
- Democracy
- Economic competitiveness
- Education

🔊 **SECOND LISTENING** europban. Fainans, un, Intraidicional.

CD 3, TR 16

Listen to the lecture again and make your notes as complete as possible.

THIRD LISTENING

🔊 Ⓐ You will hear part of the lecture again. Listen and complete the notes by adding
CD 3, TR 17   the information from the box.

| ASEAN | econ | force | Mid | NATO | wrld | & |

use os

Hard Power = threat or use of __Force__ → hard power

difindtion

• economics

sanctions

• mil

china

US role = bal of power in __world__

  - __middle__ East (free flow of oil)

  - Europe — __NATO__ (organ of Eur ntns keep peace in wrld)

  - Asia — bal bet. ASEAN __&__ China

    __ASEAN__ incld e.g. Indonesia, Malaysia

Ⓑ Compare your answers with a partner. Then compare the notes in **A** with the
notes you took for this part of the lecture.

ACCURACY CHECK

(handwritten margin notes: oral, mandy, economy, amidity, 24=30/6)

A Listen to the following questions, and write short answers. Use your notes. You will hear each question one time only.

CD 3, TR 18

(handwritten answers:)

1. ? ch 4 contries represntive by acronim BRIC? → *Brazil Russia India china*
2. wt 2 kinds of strengt in china Size? ← economi
3. Named 2 eco? 1- Ability to mintain fainacial stability. 2- Ability to help others in crisis.
4. wt ? ? ? have on china eco? → make thing more exp.
5. wt is hard-powr. / use of threat or use of force.
6. wt orgnize ds the USA belong too? NATO
7. witch orga ds Indian & Asia " ? ASEAN
8. witch 2 countris Rank #1 & #2 in the world? ┌ Britin └ France
9. A wt kind of tekno is the USA is a Leader?
10. Named 3 orgnize bisid NATO. united nation / uorepian /

(handwritten margin: nano & bayo Tiknology.)

B Check your answers with your teacher. If your score is less than 70 percent, you may need to listen to the lecture again and rewrite some of your notes.

ORAL SUMMARY

Use your notes to create an oral summary of the lecture with your partner. As you work together, add details to your notes that your partner included but you had missed.

DISCUSSION

Discuss the following questions with a classmate or in a small group.

1. Which of the four BRIC nations, besides China, is most likely to be the next superpower?

2. Would the world be a safer place if the United States were less powerful?

3. In what ways are economic sanctions *→ prohibited.* preferable to military force?

4. What are the advantages of having more than one superpower in the world? What are the disadvantages?

(handwritten margin: Keep guard → watch-ful.)

PRE-READING

The following Reading is about China's rapid economic growth. Before you read, answer the following questions. Share your answers with a classmate.

1. Look at the title of the article. What do you think "Go Green" means?

2. Scan the article for sentences that mention the United States. What comparisons does the writer make between the United States and China?

READING

Now read the article.

Can China Go Green?

Rizhao, in Shandong Province, is one of the hundreds of Chinese cities beginning to really grow. The road into town is eight-lanes wide, even though at the moment there's not much traffic. But the port is very busy. A big sign tells the residents to "build a civilized city and be a civilized citizen."

Rizhao is the kind of place that has scientists around the world deeply worried—China's rapid growth and new wealth are pushing carbon emissions higher and higher. It's the kind of growth that has led China to pass the United States to become the world's largest source of global warming gases.

And yet, after lunch at the Guangdian Hotel, the city's chief engineer, Yu Haibo, led me to the roof of the restaurant for another view. First we climbed over the hotel's solar-thermal system, a system that takes the sun's energy and turns it into all the hot water the kitchen and 102 rooms can possibly use. Then, from the edge of the roof, we looked at the view of the spreading skyline. On top of every single building a similar solar system could be seen. Solar is in at least 95 percent of all the buildings, Yu said proudly. "Some people say 99 percent, but I'm shy to say that."

Whatever the percentage, it's impressive—outside Honolulu, no city in the United States even comes close. China now leads the planet in energy produced by renewable solar and wind energy sources.

So, which is true? Is China the world's largest producer of global warming gases? Or is it the world's largest producer of renewable energy? The truth is, it's both. Here's what we know: China is growing faster than any other big country has ever grown before, and that growth is opening real opportunities for environmental progress. Because it's putting up so many new buildings and power plants, the country can incorporate the latest technology more easily than countries with more mature economies. It's not just solar and wind energy. Some 25 Chinese cities are putting in subway systems or adding to existing ones. High-speed rail tracks are spreading in every direction. But all that growth takes lots of steel and cement, and as a result pours carbon into the air, which overwhelms the environmental progress. According to many energy experts, China's carbon emissions will continue to rise until at least 2030. This means that environmental progress in China will probably come too late to prevent more dramatic global warming, which could lead to environmental disasters such as the melting of the Himalayan glaciers and the rise of the seas.

It's a dark picture. Changing it in any real way will require change beyond China—most important, some kind of international agreement involving economies that use the most carbon—including of course the United States. At the moment China is taking steps that make sense for both the environment and its economy. "Why would they want to waste energy?" Deborah Seligsohn of the World Resources Institute asked, adding that "if the U.S. changed the game in a fundamental way—if it really committed to dramatic reductions—then China would look beyond its domestic interests and perhaps go much further." But for the moment, China's growth will continue, a roaring fire that throws off green sparks but burns with dangerous heat.

DISCUSSION

Discuss these questions with a classmate.

1. How is the focus of the lecture different from the focus of the article? Are there topics in the reading that are not mentioned in the lecture? Are there topics in the lecture that are not mentioned in the reading?

2. Do you think the author of the article would agree with the lecturer's view of the importance of the United States as a global power? Why or why not?

3. Do you think the lecturer would agree with the author of the article about the importance of China as a global power? Why or why not?

PURSUING THE TOPIC

Explore the topic of this chapter further by doing the following.

Watch a short YouTube video in which Professor Joseph Nye from Harvard's Kennedy School of Government speaks to Knoowii TV about the use of hard power, soft power, and smart power in international relations. Be prepared to discuss the ideas in the video with your classmates.

www.youtube.com/watch?v=cH9hn3_Q4qQ

UNIT 3
VIDEO

My Journey in the Muslim World

BEFORE VIEWING

TOPIC PREVIEW

Alexandra Avakian is a photojournalist. She was asked to take photographs of Muslims living in the United States. Answer the following questions with a partner.

1. What images or scenes would you expect to see in her photographs?

2. What different types of people would you expect to see in her photographs?

3. Do you think that Muslims in America have more or fewer difficulties than other immigrants living in the United States? Why or why not?

VOCABULARY PREVIEW

A Read the definitions of these key words and phrases that you will hear during the video.

engaged in actively involved in or part of something

an expert a person having a lot of knowledge about a particular topic

post 9/11 after the September 11, 2001, attack on the United States

fled left an area quickly in order to escape danger

reflected shown on a surface such as a mirror; seen in a person's expression

mainstream average; usual for the typical people in a group

are converting to are changing from one belief system, such as a religion, to a new one

maximum-security prison a prison where the most dangerous criminals are kept

protective keeping someone or something safe from harm

B Work with a partner and write in the blank the word from the box that completes the sentence.

artistic	civil war	pressure	security
Catholics	granddaughter	relatives	village

1. The _____ she was under was **reflected** in her face.

2. The man was not an **expert** photographer, but his photos were very _____.

3. The _____ were very **protective** of their young _____.

4. **Post 9/11**, there has been increased _____ at U.S. airports.

5. There are **mainstream** _____ who **are converting to** Islam.

6. The whole _____ was very **engaged in** preparations for the fair.

7. Some people **fled** during the _____; others were placed in a **maximum-security prison**.

VIEWING

🖥 FIRST VIEWING

Watch the video, and then compare your first impressions with a partner. Talk about what you remember, what surprised you, and what interested you.

🖥 SECOND VIEWING

Watch the video again. Listen for the missing words and write them in the blanks.

1. I hope to _____ a wider view of a group of people much misunderstood, especially _____ 9/11.

2. And these are Ryazan _____, and they're an alternative, Islamic alternative to Barbie.

3. And you know Muslim Americans, like all Americans, have fled civil war, dictatorship, _____ hardship.

4. These are Persian Americans, Iranian Americans, and they jump over _____ on their New Year to cast off the bad luck of the previous year, you know, for good luck in the _____ year.

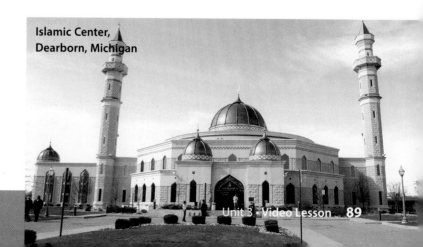

Islamic Center, Dearborn, Michigan

Complete these notes as you watch the video. Write only important words, not full sentences, and abbreviate common words.

Book = not all Ms
- not an expt.
- about misunderstood ppl after 9/11

Photos:
1) Dolls
2) Ldy fled CW:
3) Latif M. and Flo M.:
4) Zulia:
5) Penn.
6) Los Angeles:

AFTER VIEWING

ORAL SUMMARY

Use your notes to create an oral summary of the video with your partner. As you work together, add details to your notes that your partner included but you had missed.

DISCUSSION

Discuss the following questions with a classmate or in a small group.

1. What information about Alexandra Avakian's personal life do you learn during her lecture?

2. The speaker says that Muslims are a "group of people much misunderstood." What do you think makes her feel this way?

3. Which of the photos of Muslim Americans most interested you? Explain.

Public Education in the United States

TOPIC PREVIEW

Discuss the following questions with a partner or your classmates.

1. Are children in your country of origin required to attend school? If so, until what age?

2. How are public schools in your country of origin funded, that is, where does the money come from to run the schools?

3. Where do most parents in your country of origin prefer to send their children: private schools or public schools? Why?

A student gets off the school bus in McCool Junction, Nebraska.

VOCABULARY PREVIEW

compulsory.

🔊 CD 4, TR 1

A Read through the sentences below, which are missing vocabulary from the lecture. As you read, try to imagine which words would fit in the blanks. Then listen to the sentences and write the missing words in the blanks.

1. In the United States, attending school is _compulsory_ —children have to attend school, in most states to the age of 16.

2. A small percentage of American students attend private schools, either religious or _secular_ . *secular → non religious.*

3. One unusual feature of U.S. public education is that there is no nationwide _curriculum_ set by the federal government. And, there are no particular nationwide _standardized_ examinations.

4. Although the _federal_ government provides _funds_ to schools for special programs, it does *not* determine the curriculum or the examinations.

5. The state sets the number of _credits_ a student must complete in order to graduate high school, and the credits include both required courses and _electives_ .

6. The school board is _elected_ by the citizens of the district or _appointed_ by local officials.

7. Because private schools are not funded from taxes, parents pay _tuition_ to send their children to them.

8. The basic idea behind school _vouchers_ is that parents choose the school their children will attend—public or private—and that school receives a set amount of money per student from public school funds.

9. Voucher schools are usually private schools, which are usually _affiliated_ with religious organizations.

10. Congress passed an education bill called No Child Left Behind (NCLB), which required each state to develop and _implement_ testing programs.

B Check the spelling of the vocabulary words with your teacher. Discuss the meanings of these words and any other unfamiliar words in the sentences.

PREDICTIONS

Think about the questions in the Topic Preview on page 92 and the sentences you heard in the Vocabulary Preview. Write three questions that you think will be answered in the lecture. Share your questions with your classmates.

NOTETAKING PREPARATION

Using Outline Form with Letters and Numbers

You have already practiced organizing your notes by writing the most important information to the left and less important information to the right. As you develop this skill, you can use numbers and letters to make the organization even clearer. You can use Roman numerals (I, II, etc.); capital letters; Arabic numerals (1, 2, etc.); and small letters to identify the levels of detail, from general to specific, in an outline. For example:

I. Economic reasons for U.S. remaining a global player
    A. Enough money to help others in a crisis
        1. natural disasters
            a. tsunami
            b. volcanic eruption
        2. countries in bad financial situation
        3. countries with political problems
    B. U.S. helps maintain stability as a market for the world's goods

A **Look at the lecture notes in the box above. Answer the questions about the notes by writing the letters or numerals of the correct notes.**

1. Which point in the outline is the most general, that is, the main idea?

    _____I_____

2. Which points explain the main idea?

    _____A_____
    _____B_____

3. Which points give a third level of detail about the main idea?

    _____1_____
    _____2_____
    _____3_____

4. Which points are specific examples?

    _____a_____
    _____b_____

B Listen to part of the lecture. Write notes to complete the outline below. Some information is already filled in for you. Fill in the rest of the information as you listen.

I. Three levels of control within states
  A. _state department of edu_
    1. Responsibilities
      a. Sets curriculum requirements
      b. _sets the number of credit._
  B. School district
    1. Numbers depend on _~~size~~ state & population_
    2. School board is elected or appointed
    3. Responsibilities
      a. _specific content._
        i. required courses
        ii. _electivs._
      b. _hairing teachers._
  C. _school._ (Individal.)
    1. Teachers' responsibilities
      a. _How to teach each corse._
      b. _giveing examintion._

C Discourse Cues Number the following excerpts from the lecture from 1 to 5 in the order that you think you will probably hear them. Discuss with a partner or as a class the discourse cues that helped you figure out the order.

__2__ The first issue is inequality of educational opportunity.

__5__ Let's talk first about charter schools.

__1__ Today, I'd like to discuss two educational issues and efforts to solve them.

__3__ The second issue involves private schools.

__4__ Two efforts to deal with these issues are charter schools and school vouchers.

appropiate. ✓

FIRST LISTENING

🔊 CD 4, TR 3

A Listen to the beginning of the lecture. Circle the set of notes below that best records the information you hear.

a.

I. School Compul in US
  A. 16 or 9th gr
  B. K–12
  C. Pub schl
    1. 90% sec
  D. Priv schl
    2. rel/sec
II. US pub ed
  A. No ntl curric & exams
  B. Spec prgs-hndcp, biling
  C. States contrl
    1. 3 levels
    2. Funding
    3. Issues & efforts

b.

US public schools — intro
  A. Compul. (must att) to age 16 or gr 9
  B. fr K/1st (age 5/6) to 12th gr (18) = "K through 12"
  C. 90% stud in pub. sch; sm no. priv sch.
    1. priv, relig or secu; pub, all secu
  ②—⟨D. No national curric or exams⟩
    1. Fed gov. fund special prog
      a. handicap
      b. bilingual
Control of ed by indiv states (today)
I. 3 levels of contrl w/in a state
II. How ed funded
III. Issues + efforts (st & nat) to fix

🔊 CD 4, TR 4

B Now listen to the whole lecture and take notes. Look at the lecturer's visual aids as you listen. These may help you understand parts of the lecture.

Subtopic 1: Three Levels of Control in Each State

control become local.

sets the

student have to complet edu. 70 graduate

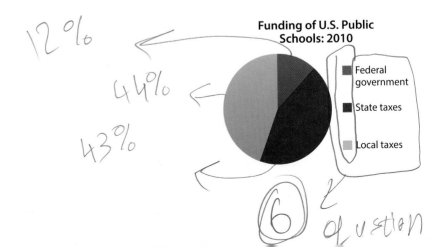

State Department of Education
School Districts / School Boards
Schools / Teachers

Subtopic 2: How Ed. Is Funded

12%
44%
43%

Funding of U.S. Public Schools: 2010
■ Federal government
■ State taxes
▨ Local taxes

⑥ ? of uestion

Subtopic 3: _Ed. Issues & Efforts to Solve Them_

PuP. school don't have rhathones that
wealthy school

Poivet school.

ore esfforts zosolve

Issues and Solutions

Inequality of Educational Opportunity
- Charter schools
- School vouchers

PuPlicK _privet_

Educational Standards
- No Child Left Behind (NCLB)
- Common Core State Standards (CCSS)

oyustion 8

hud crisize

ovustion. establish npw goals

Eng math.

CD 4, TR 5

SECOND LISTENING   _stardors &_

Listen to the lecture again and make your notes as complete as possible.

THIRD LISTENING

CD 4, TR 6

A You will hear part of the lecture again. Listen and complete the notes by adding the information from the box.

AY	critics	pub	Ss	↑	>	??	$$

A. Chart Schs = type _____ sch
   1. funding fr taxes
   2. compt w/ reg pub schls for _____
   3. operate
      a. chrtr/contr fr St/lcl sch bd/oth pub org
      b. _____ indep
         - selectng Ts
         - curric
         - _____
   4. CSs–Stats
      a. 1st @ end 1980s
      b. AY 1999/2000 → 2009/10 # Ss ↑ fr 0.3M to 1.6M (4X _____)
      c. _____ 2009/10 CSs = ~5% of all pub sch's
   5. effective _____ — studies mixed
   6. _____ fear CSs mngd by priv comp's w/ intrst in $$ not ed

B Compare your answers with a partner. Then compare the notes in **A** with the notes you took for this part of the lecture.

A+ wt 3 control in edu

ACCURACY CHECK

🔊
CD 4, TR 7

A Listen to the following questions and write short answers. Use your notes. You will hear each question one time only.

1. ~~How~~ old
2. wt 2 things R suprising about Am. systim.
3. wt 3 things of control in the U.S.A.
4. WI 1 type of disaction.
5. How R the ppl in school bord choosen.
6. wt R 3 ways
7. How did pup. school funded
8. wt is the diff betwen charter & vocchers
9. wt is main objection. / No child left behind. *school?*
10. wt is Name of the national evets.

elected apointed
B/c of taxes
(CSS)

B Check your answers with your teacher. If your score is less than 70 percent, you may need to listen to the lecture again and rewrite some of your notes.

ORAL SUMMARY

Use your notes to create an oral summary of the lecture with your partner. As you work together, add details to your notes that your partner included but you did not.

DISCUSSION

Discuss the following questions with a classmate or in a small group.

1. Should people who don't have children attending public schools have to pay the same taxes as people who do? Why or why not?

2. Should all children nationwide be receiving exactly the same education? Why or why not?

3. What other reasons besides less funding for schools in poor areas might also contribute to poorer educational outcomes?

4. Would you send your children to a public school or a private school? Why?

PRE-READING

The following Reading is about pressures faced by Chinese school children.
Before you read, answer the following questions. Share your answers with
a classmate.

1. Look at the title of the Reading article. What is prosperity? Anxiety? What types of
   anxieties might sudden prosperity bring?

2. In what ways do you think the lives of school children can be affected by a country's
   rapid economic growth?

READING

Now read the article.

successful

China's Sudden Prosperity Brings New Freedoms and Anxieties

worried

spical

some thing old

The past decade has seen the rise of a Chinese middle class, now estimated to number between 100 million and 150 million people. These days, Chinese people are free to choose where to live, work, and travel, and economic opportunities grow year by year. However, if you pick up a Chinese newspaper, what comes through is a sense of discomfort at the speed of social change. Parents struggle to teach their children but feel their own knowledge is out of date. Children often guide their parents through the complications of modern life. "Society has completely turned around," says Zhou Xiaohong, a sociologist at Nanjing University. "Fathers used to give orders, but now fathers listen to their sons."

Because their parents have such high hopes for them, children are among the most pressured. They live in a world that combines old and new, with the most punishing elements of both. The traditional examination system that selects a favored few for higher education remains: The number of students started on the piano, which taught discipline and developed the brain. In the summers she went to the pool for lessons; swimming, her parents said, would make her taller. Bella wanted to be a lawyer, and to be a lawyer you had to be tall.

By the time she was 10, Bella lived a life that was rich with possibility and as strictly regulated as a soldier's. After school she did homework until her parents got home. Then came dinner, bath, piano practice. Sometimes she was permitted television, but only the news. On Saturdays she took a private essay class followed by Math Olympics, and on Sundays a piano lesson and a prep class for her entrance exam to a Shanghai middle school. The best moment of the week was Friday afternoon, when school let out early. Bella might take a deep breath and look around, like a man who discovers a glimpse of blue sky from the prison yard. *brif look*

The effort to shape Bella is full of contradictions. Her parents encourage her independence but worry that school and the workplace will punish her for it. They are concerned about how much homework she has, but they then add more assignments on top of her regular schoolwork. "We don't want to be brutal to her," says Bella's father, Zhou Jiliang. "But in China, the environment doesn't let you do anything else."

oppisit. sids opposition.

entering college in a given year is equal to 11 percent of the college-freshman-age population, compared with 64 percent in the United States. Yet the desire to develop well-rounded students has also led to an explosion of activities—music lessons, English, drawing, and martial arts classes—all of which are highly competitive.

→ any year mentiond

The life of Zhou Jiaying, a Chinese girl from Shanghai, is typical. At the age of four, Zhou Jiaying was enrolled in two classes—Spoken American English and English Conversation—and given the English name Bella. Her parents hoped she might go abroad for college. When she turned eight, she

DISCUSSION

Discuss these questions with a classmate.

1. Do you think Bella goes to a public school or a private school? Use specific information from the reading and the lecture as well as your own knowledge to explain your answer.

2. Compare and contrast the information in the lecture and Reading about the importance of standardized testing in schools in the United States and China.

3. In what ways are Bella's experiences similar to those of an American school child? In what ways are they different?

PURSUING THE TOPIC

Explore the topic of this chapter further by doing the following.

Watch the movie *The Joy Luck Club*, a 1993 movie about the lives of four immigrant Chinese mothers raising their daughters in San Francisco. Be prepared to discuss the movie with your classmates.

CHAPTER 11

The College Admissions Process

TOPIC PREVIEW

Discuss the following questions with a partner or your classmates.

1. In your culture, what is the most important exam that a high school student takes?

2. What happens if students do not do well on the exam?

3. How difficult is it to be admitted to a university in your culture? Why?

Students taking an exam in a college lecture hall

VOCABULARY PREVIEW

🔊
CD 4, TR 8

(A) Read through the sentences below, which are missing vocabulary from the lecture. As you read, try to imagine which words would fit in the blanks. Then listen to the sentences and write the missing words in the blanks.

1. Most colleges are _____, which means the schools meet certain standards set by outside _____.

2. Over three-quarters of all students—76 percent—are _____ in public colleges and universities.

3. The average cost in 2012 for tuition and room and board at a four-year college for a student living on _____ in a _____ varies a lot.

4. With such a wide variety of schools of different sizes, types, and locations, it probably won't surprise you to find out that admissions _____ at these colleges and universities can vary, too.

5. Four-year colleges and universities will all require an _____ and a high school _____, which is a record of the applicant's grades and rank in their high school class.

6. Very often applicants for an _____ program must also include an essay and recommendations from high school teachers

7. Some people say standardized exams don't fairly evaluate a student's _____ for college.

8. Even the most _____ and most highly competitive colleges and universities will consider other factors.

9. Admissions standards at community colleges are usually more _____ than those at four-year colleges and universities.

10. Many community college programs are vocational in nature, that is, they train students to become medical technicians, office assistants, cooks, airline mechanics, or other _____ workers needed by the community.

11. Students in the United States have many _____ in pursuing higher education.

(B) Check the spelling of the vocabulary words with your teacher. Discuss the meanings of these words and any other unfamiliar words in the sentences.

PREDICTIONS

Think about the questions in the Topic Preview on page 101 and the sentences you heard in the Vocabulary Preview. Write three questions that you think will be answered in the lecture. Share your questions with your classmates.

NOTETAKING PREPARATION

Acronyms and Abbreviations 2

You have learned that acronyms are words formed by the first letters of the words in the name of something and are pronounced as words, not individual letters. For example, IELTS (International English Language Testing System) is an acronym and it is pronounced /ˈaɪ.ɛlts/.

Abbreviations like EFL (English as a Foreign Language) and ESL (English as a Second Language) are different because they are pronounced letter by letter (E-F-L; E-S-L). Some other short forms are a combination—part abbreviation and part acronym. For example, MCAT (Medical College Admission Test) is pronounced M-cat, like the letter M and the word cat.

CD 4, TR 9

A **Listen to a part of the lecture. Write the short form—abbreviation, acronym, or combination—that you hear next to what it represents.**

1. Standardized admission tests for college _____ _____

2. Standardized admission test for many graduate schools _____

3. Graduate business degree program _____

4. Standardized admission test for graduate business school _____

5. Standardized admission test for law school _____

6. Standardized English-language exams required of foreign students

_____ _____

B **Discourse Cues** **Number the following excerpts from the lecture from 1 to 5 in the order that you think you will probably hear them. Discuss with a partner or as a class the discourse cues that helped you figure out the order.**

_____ With such a wide variety of schools of different sizes, types, and locations, it probably won't surprise you to find out that admissions requirements at these colleges and universities can vary, too.

_____ Let's begin with some facts and figures.

_____ In this lecture, I'm going to talk to you about postsecondary education in the United States, that is, education that students pursue after high school.

_____ Very often applicants for an undergraduate program must also include an essay and recommendations from high school teachers with their application.

_____ In brief, you can see that educational opportunities and admissions standards at postsecondary schools vary greatly in the United States.

FIRST LISTENING

CD 4, TR 10

A Listen to the beginning of the lecture. Circle the set of notes below that best records the information you hear.

a.

Postsecondary Ed in US
  I. Facts and figures
  II. Gen info abt admiss
       policies
  III. Comm Coll

b.

Postsecondary Ed in US =
HS Ed
Most coll accrdtd (outside
eval standrds)
  1. Gen info abt admiss
     policies
  2. Community Coll

c.

  I. Postsecondary Ed in US
  II. Facts and Figures
  III. Gen info abt admiss
       policies
  IV. Commun Coll

CD 4, TR 11

B Now listen to the whole lecture and take notes. Look at the lecturer's visual aids as you listen. These may help you understand parts of the lecture.

Subtopic 1: _____

Colleges & Universities
▪ Private vs. public
▪ Size
▪ Student body
▪ Programs of study
▪ Location
▪ Cost

Subtopic 2: _____

Requirements
▪ Application
▪ Standardized tests
▪ Diversity
▪ High school rank

Subtopic 3: _____

🔊
CD 4, TR 12

SECOND LISTENING

Listen to the lecture again and make your notes as complete as possible.

THIRD LISTENING

🔊
CD 4, TR 13

A You will hear part of the lecture again. Listen and complete the notes by adding the information from the box.

| HS | req | Ss | Ts | IELTS | LSAT | SAT |

II. Admissions: _____ vary dep on type—2-yr coll few req, but 4-yr req:
   A. Application
      1. _____ transcript
      2. Undergrad — essay + rec fr HS _____
   B. Standardized tests
      1. Undergrad: _____ & ACT
      2. Grad: GRE, GMAT (for MBA), _____ (for law)
      3. Foreign _____: TOEFL, _____

B Compare your answers with a partner. Then compare the notes in **A** with the notes you took for this part of the lecture.

ACCURACY CHECK

🔊
CD 4, TR 14

A Listen to the following questions and write short answers. Use your notes. You will hear each question one time only.

1. _____
2. _____
3. _____
4. _____
5. _____
6. _____
7. _____
8. _____
9. _____
10. _____

B Check your answers with your teacher. If your score is less than 70 percent, you may need to listen to the lecture again and rewrite some of your notes.

ORAL SUMMARY

Use your notes to create an oral summary of the lecture with your partner. As you work together, add details to your notes that your partner included but you had missed.

DISCUSSION

Discuss the following questions with a classmate or in a small group.

1. What are the advantages and disadvantages of a highly competitive examination system that limits the number of students who can enter the university?

2. What are the advantages and disadvantages of a less competitive system that allows more students to continue their education after secondary school?

3. In your opinion, which should college admissions officers look at more carefully: a student's transcript, extra-curricular activities, teacher recommendations, or standardized test scores?

PRE-READING

The following Reading is about a global ranking of higher education systems. Before you read, answer the following questions. Share your answers with a classmate.

1. Look at the table at the beginning of the article. Are you surprised by the rankings? Are there any countries missing that you expected to find? Explain.

2. What types of information do you think the authors of the report used to determine the rankings?

READING

Now read the article.

International Ranking of Systems of Higher Education

Universitas 21 (U21) is a global network of universities. Its purpose is to promote global citizenship through international research collaboration. In May 2012, U21 released a report containing the first international ranking of higher education systems, a project carried out at the Institute of Applied Economic and Social Reasearch at the University of Melbourne. Forty-eight countries were included. Four variables were considered in determining the rankings: resources, environment, connectivity, and output. The top 10 countries overall are listed in the table.

Resources include the amount of money spent on higher education, per country and per student. This is money spent on educating students and conducting research. It includes money spent by the government, private citizens, businesses, and the educational institutions themselves. The country that spent the most on higher education was Canada, followed by Denmark, Sweden, and the United States. It is interesting to note that Great Britain, the country that ranked tenth overall, ranked quite low in this category, twenty-seventh.

The second category, environment, includes an evaluation of government regulations on higher education. In particular, the authors were looking at measures to ensure quality education and to what

U21 Rankings 2012		
RANK	COUNTRY	SCORE
1	United States	100.0
2	Sweden	83.6
3	Canada	82.8
4	Finland	82.0
5	Denmark	81.0
6	Switzerland	80.3
7	Norway	78.0
8	Australia	77.8
9	Netherlands	77.4
10	United Kingdom	76.8

degree government regulations restricted academic freedom. Included under environment are variables such as the number of female students and academic staff as compared to male students and staff, the availability of government data on higher education, and information about governmental control over the selection of academic staff at individual institutions. The Netherlands came out on top in this category, with New Zealand and the United States coming in second and third.

The third category, connectivity, measures interaction with institutes of higher education in other countries. It takes into account the number of international students enrolled in higher education in the country and the number of articles coauthored with collaborators from other countries. Austria, Singapore, and Australia were ranked as the top three countries. Interestingly, the United States was not among the top 10 countries in this category. According to the report's authors, this is because so many top research institutions are located within the United States.

The final category, output, looks at three things. First, does the higher education system provide the country with a workforce educated to meet the country's needs? Second, does it provide opportunities to people with different interests and skills? Finally, does it contribute to national and world knowledge? Output takes into account, among other things, the number of academic researchers and the number of articles produced, per country and per student; the quality of the research produced; the percentage of the population enrolled in higher education; and unemployment rates of people with degrees from institutions of higher education. In output, the United States came out on top, followed by the United Kingdom, Canada, Finland, and Sweden.

It is interesting that some neighboring countries had similar overall rankings. For example, the Eastern European countries of Ukraine, the Czech Republic, Poland, and Slovenia ranked between 25 and 28. The Latin American countries of Chile, Argentina, Brazil, and Mexico also ranked close together. The report's authors say, "It would seem that while many countries may feel they cannot hope to match the higher education system in the United States, they do want to match that of their neighbors."

DISCUSSION

Discuss these questions with a classmate.

1. What information from the lecture would you include for each of the variables discussed in the article—resources, environment, connectivity, and output? Make a list on a separate paper.

2. Think about what you learned from the lecture and the article. Why do you think the United States has a highly regarded system of higher education?

3. How is the system of higher education in the United States different from the system of higher education in your country or in another country with which you are familiar?

PURSUING THE TOPIC

Explore the topic of this chapter further by doing the following.

Individually or with a partner, look at the most recent U21 ranking of national higher education systems at the following Web address. Choose a topic or country that interests you and read more about it. Write up the details for a short presentation to the class.

www.universitas21.com/article/projects/details/152/u21-ranking-of-national-higher-education-systems

CHAPTER 12

International Students

TOPIC PREVIEW

Discuss the following questions with a partner or your classmates.

1. Which countries do you think most postsecondary international students in the United States come from?

2. What do you suppose are the most popular fields of study for these international students?

3. What benefits do you think these international students bring to their new U.S. college or university?

[handwritten top margin: pumb → مضخة / sight → your vision]

[handwritten: net worth → الثروة كما صافي]

VOCABULARY PREVIEW

A Read through the sentences below, which are missing vocabulary from the lecture. As you read, try to imagine which words would fit in the blanks. Then listen to the sentences and write the missing words in the blanks.

[handwritten left margin: constatly / باستمرار]

1. The number of international students studying in the United States has risen quite ___**steadily**___ over the last 50 to 60 years, with an occasional small ___**dip**___ due to political or economic reasons.

[handwritten left margin: هبوط]
[handwritten right margin: رتفاع / → rise]

2. In number of students, China only recently ___**surged**___ ahead of India, which had been number one for most of the previous decade.

3. Social sciences include such ___**disciblien s**___ as sociology, psychology, and political science.

[handwritten: حقول]

4. Building "bridges," or relationships, between the United States and other countries, and bringing global ways of looking at things are the types of benefits ___**virtually**___ everyone mentions when talking about students going to different countries to study.

[handwritten left margin: almost - always.]

5. As one benefit, NAFSA, an association of international educators, ___**site**___ the contribution international students make with their local spending on shopping, housing, and so forth.

[handwritten left margin: place]

6. In the academic year of 2010–2011, international students and their families made a ___**net**___ contribution to the U.S. economy of about 20 billion dollars.

7. Some criticisms have been raised about ___**policies**___ that encourage not only the admission of so many international students, especially to graduate schools, but also ones that encourage some of these students to remain after completing their degrees.

8. According to NAFSA, international students have only increased the size of Ph.D. programs, not taken ___**away**___ places from U.S. students.

9. Employers do not have to pay some taxes for certain foreign employees that they would have to pay for American employees, which critics believe is an unfair economic ___**incentive**___ to hire foreign graduates.

[handwritten: → encoregment.]

B Check the spelling of the vocabulary words with your teacher. Discuss the meanings of these words and any other unfamiliar words in the sentences.

PREDICTIONS

Think about the questions in the Topic Preview on page 109 and the sentences you heard in the Vocabulary Preview. Write three questions that you think will be answered in the lecture. Share your questions with your classmates.

NOTETAKING PREPARATION

Reviewing Basic Notetaking Skills

No two people will take exactly the same notes on any lecture. However, most people will use at least some of the same skills, such as abbreviating words, using conventional symbols, and organizing information in a way that shows main ideas and details. This means that if you miss a class and have to review a classmate's notes, you should be able to interpret them, even if the classmate uses a slightly different system of notetaking from yours.

A Read and interpret the notes below that a classmate took during a lecture on distance education. As you read, think about what abbreviations such as *Int'd*, *req*, *trad*, *disc*, and *ind* would mean.

Classmate's notes

Intrested

Destance Education.

6 Things for P'ple Int'd in DE to Consid

(1)

programs   *residentcy*

1. many DE progs have res reqs → *req wirments*

2. DE courses & progs have ti limits

time

3. DE adm's reqs = on-campus reqs

addmishins

4. DE can save $ sometimes

- Don't need to travel to class
- But academic fees = trad ed
- Res reqs can be costly

compouter

5. Online DE means stud. needs access to comp w/ min reqs

— e.g., latest version of Windows

— a microph, snd card & speakers

— adequate hard drive & RAM, modem, browser, & Internet

— Connection speed very imp

— cable modem

— DSL   → *disceblent*

6. Stud need to be disc & ind → *Indpendent.*

- DE not easier than trad ed
- dropout rate > than trad ed

B Now complete the homework assignment. Use your classmate's notes to answer the homework questions.

Homework assignment

1. Do all distance education programs have a residency requirement?

   Yes. B/c ①

2. Do DE students have to follow a timetable similar to on-campus students?

   Yes. No

3. Is it easier to be admitted to a distance program than to an on-campus programs?

   Cciowl.

4. What is the main way DS can save a student money?

   4   _3 points_

5. What are three examples of computer requirements that online study might require?

   5   _Points_

6. Is distance education easier than traditional education (i.e., on campus)?

7. Are students more likely to complete distance education programs or traditional programs?

C **Discourse Cues** Number the following excerpts from the lecture from 1 to 5 in the order that you think you will probably hear them. Discuss with a partner or as a class the discourse cues that helped you figure out the order.

_____ OK, let's begin with the number of international students studying in the United States.

_____ Well, we've covered a lot today. I hope I've at least given you some food for thought about the impact that international students have.

_____ Next I would like to discuss the benefits these students bring to the States, according to NAFSA, an association of international educators.

_____ Today I'd like to spend some time discussing international students—in this case, students from other countries studying at U.S. colleges and universities.

_____ NAFSA also addresses some of the criticisms that have been raised about policies that encourage the admission of so many international students.

FIRST LISTENING

CD 4, TR 16

Listen to the lecture and take notes. Look at the lecturer's visual aids as you listen. These may help you understand parts of the lecture.

Introduction

> **International Students**
>
> Introduction
> Facts and figures
> Benefits from foreign students
> Three criticisms

Subtopic 1: _____

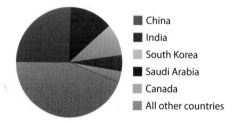

**International Students
Place of Origin, AY 2011/2012**

- China
- India
- South Korea
- Saudi Arabia
- Canada
- All other countries

Subtopic 2: _____

> **Five Benefits**
>
> 1. Building bridges
> 2. Global perspective
> 3. Science & engineering courses
> 4. Tuition income
> 5. Local spending

Subtopic 3: _____

Three Criticisms
1. Compete with U.S. students for admission
2. Compete with U.S. citizens for jobs
3. Brain drain

SECOND LISTENING

Listen to the lecture again and make your notes as complete as possible.

THIRD LISTENING

A You will hear part of the lecture again. Listen and complete the notes by adding the information from the box.

Areas	Comp	Eng	Manag	Phys	Soc	Sc

C. Interntl Ss— _____ of Study
   1. Bus & _____
   2. _____
   3. Math & _____ Sc
   4. _____ (phys, chem, astron) & Life _____, (biol, microbiol, biochem)
   5. _____ Sc (soc, psych, pol sc)

B Compare your answers with a partner. Then compare the notes in **A** with the notes you took for this part of the lecture.

⋀ᴹ

ACCURACY CHECK

CD 4, TR 19 **A** Listen to the following questions and write short answers. Use your notes. You will hear each question one time only.

1. _____
2. _____
3. _____
4. _____
5. _____
6. _____
7. _____
8. _____
9. _____
10. _____

B Check your answers with your teacher. If your score is less than 70 percent, you may need to listen to the lecture again and rewrite some of your notes.

ORAL SUMMARY

Use your notes to create an oral summary of the lecture with your partner. As you work together, add details to your notes that your partner included but you had missed.

DISCUSSION

Discuss the following questions with a classmate or in a small group.

1. What are the most important benefits of having international students in a school?

2. Looking ahead 20 years, where do you think most international students in the United States will come from? Why?

3. How would you advise a young person from your culture to study: (a) at home, at a university; (b) in the United States; (c) at home through distance education? Explain.

4. If you were a university or ministry of education official in your culture, would you try to attract more international students? Why or why not?

PRE-READING

The following Reading is about American university students studying abroad. Before you read, answer the following questions. Share your answers with a classmate.

1. Look at the chart of the top five countries hosting American students. Why do you think these five countries are at the top of the list?

2. Are there any countries missing from the list that you would expect to find there? Which?

READING

Now read the article.

Rising Numbers of Americans Study Abroad

According to the 2012 Open Doors Report on International Educational Exchange, in academic year 2011–2012 the number of Americans studying for academic credit at foreign universities rose by about 1 percent to an all-time high of 273,996. This increase, although small, is a part of a two-decades-long trend in which the total number of U.S. students participating in study-abroad programs has more than tripled.

This upward trend is welcomed by many political, business, and education leaders, who believe that in order for the United States to remain competitive in an increasingly global economy, young Americans must become more globally aware. Groups with an interest in promoting study-abroad programs speak of a "global divide" emerging between those with access to a global education and those whose education is more traditionally focused in and on the United States. They compare this to the so-called digital divide of the last decade between people who had access to personal computers and those who did not.

Commenting on the importance of a global education, U.S. Assistant Secretary of State for Educational and Cultural Affairs Ann Stock said, "Today's youth are tomorrow's leaders. International education creates strong, lasting relationships between the U.S. and emerging leaders worldwide. Students return home with new perspectives and a global skill set that will allow them to build more prosperous, stable societies."

According to the International Institute on Education (IIE), out of the 25 most popular study abroad destinations for American university students, 17 countries reported an increase in American participants in 2011–2012. The most popular region for study abroad participants remains Europe, with 54.6%, followed by Latin America with 14.6%, and Asia with 11.7%. In 2011–2012, there were increases in several less traditional destinations, including Brazil, China, Costa Rica, India, and South Korea, with particularly significant increases from the previous year in India (up 12%) and China (up 5% to 14,000 students).

In 2010, during a trip to China, President Obama set a goal of doubling the number of Americans studying in that country by 2014. While this goal was praised by organizations committed to study abroad programs, some experts criticized it as being too ambitious. One criticism is that the president has not committed any government funding to achieve this goal, which the U.S. State Department estimates

Top Five Countries Hosting U.S. Students, 2011/12

1. United Kingdom
2. Italy
3. Spain
4. France
5. China

Oxford University, England

would cost at least $68 million. So far, American corporations have committed $3.25 million according to Carola McGiffert, director of the initiative. Another challenge is that very few U.S. universities have the language programs in place to prepare American students to function in classrooms where only Chinese is spoken. In addition to increasing the number of Chinese language courses, American universities will need to increase course offerings in Chinese literature, history, political science, and economics. "Otherwise, the study-abroad experience just isn't connected to a student's broader educational experience," Brian J. Whalen, president of the Forum on Education Abroad, said.

DISCUSSION

Discuss these questions with a classmate.

1. Compare the information in the Reading with what you heard in the lecture. What are the similarities and differences between Americans studying abroad at foreign universities and international students studying at American universities?

2. Why do you think President Obama was interested in increasing the number of Americans studying in China? Consider what you learned in the lecture about the benefits of international education, as well as your own ideas.

3. Based on what you learned in the lecture, what are some of the potential benefits to other countries of having Americans enrolled in their universities?

PURSUING THE TOPIC

Explore the topic of this chapter further by doing the following.

The Web site for the Institute of International Education has a lot of information on study abroad in both the United States and other countries. Individually or with a partner, choose a country or region that interests you and read about it. Write up the details for a short presentation to the class.

www.iie.org/en

UNIT 4
VIDEO
The Story of Hiram Bingham

The Inca ruins at Machu Picchu, Peru

TOPIC PREVIEW

The speaker talks about the life of Hiram Bingham. Work with a partner and number the events in Bingham's life from 1 through 6 in what you think is the most likely order.

_____ had seven sons

_____ taught Latin American history at university

_____ received a doctorate degree

_____ became an explorer

_____ went to Harvard graduate school

_____ was a freshman at Yale University

VOCABULARY PREVIEW

A Read the definitions of these key words and phrases that you will hear during the video.

heading off to college beginning study at a college, usually away from home

got into college was accepted into a college

end up finally become something after effort, time, or academic studies

senior year the final year of high school or college

advisor a person who helps students plan their academic studies

ambitious wanting to succeed and do very well, usually professionally

fellow students classmates

barrier something in your path that makes it difficult to get where you want to go

be hired be given a job for which you are paid

B Work with a partner and discuss answers to the following questions.

1. When children **head off to college**, do you think it is a difficult time for their parents?

2. Who do you know who **got into college** to study one subject but **ended up** with a degree in another subject?

3. What is a student's **senior year** of high school or college usually like? Do students usually work harder or less hard than in other years? Explain.

4. What is the role of an **advisor** at a school?

5. Do you consider yourself an **ambitious** person? What is your ambition?

6. Do you meet socially with any of your **fellow students**? If so, what do you do together?

7. What are some **barriers** for poorer people to get into a good college or to **be hired** for a well-paying job?

VIEWING

🖥 FIRST VIEWING

Watch the video, and then compare your first impressions with a partner. Talk about what you remember, what surprised you, and what interested you.

🖥 SECOND VIEWING

Watch the video again. Listen for the missing words and write them in the blanks.

Hiram Bingham

1. I mean, he's very _____; he's six feet four. He's _____. He wears jodhpurs like the best of them.

2. Hiram Bingham, in a _____, was a whirlwind. He was a force of _____.

3. There still was a barrier of both wealth and prestige at Yale that he couldn't quite _____ through.

4. Now, his decision to study _____ at Harvard was actually a fairly radical one.

5. He wasn't doing European history. He wasn't doing _____ history. He was doing _____ American history.

Complete these notes as you watch the video. Write only important words, not full sentences, and abbreviate common words.

Hiram Bingham
- striking and _____
- Yale's Ind. Jones
- whirlwind/force of nature/smart/ambitious/gd. _____
- gd at _____
- poor _____
- barriers at Y. _____
- after coll _____

Fell in love w/ Alfreda M.
- chngd his life
- met in _____
- m. soon after — 7 _____
- lvd in _____ — at Harvard

Study hist. at Harv.
- not Euro or US — _____
- 1st pers _____
- bel. _____

AFTER VIEWING

ORAL SUMMARY

Use your notes to create an oral summary of the video with your partner. As you work together, add details to your notes that your partner included but you had missed.

DISCUSSION

Discuss the following questions with a classmate or in a small group.

1. What do you think were the three most impressive achievements in Bingham's life?

2. Why was Hiram Bingham known as "Yale's Indiana Jones"?

3. The speaker says that many students "fear" moving back to their parents' house after college. Why do you think he says that and do you agree that it is something to fear?

The Official Side

Fourth of July fireworks
over Washington, DC

CHAPTER 13

The Role of Government in the Economy

TOPIC PREVIEW

Discuss the following questions with a partner or your classmates.

1. Do you think the oil fields in Texas or the oil platforms in the Gulf of Mexico are owned by the U.S. government or by private companies?

2. Are energy industries (oil, gas, electricity) privately or publicly owned in your country of origin?

3. What role should the government play if certain industries pollute the environment or try to create a monopoly by driving others out of business? No role? A big one? Why?

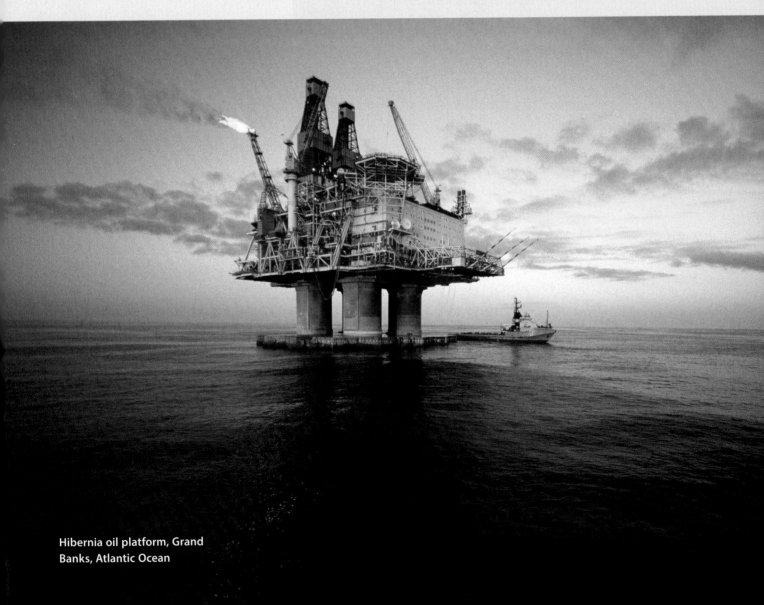

Hibernia oil platform, Grand Banks, Atlantic Ocean

VOCABULARY PREVIEW

🔊
CD 5, TR 1

A **Read through the sentences below, which are missing vocabulary from the lecture. As you read, try to imagine which words would fit in the blanks. Then listen to the sentences and write the missing words in the blanks.**

1. One of the important characteristics of American-style _____ is individual _____ of property.

2. Another important characteristic is free _____: This means the freedom to produce, buy, and sell goods and labor without government _____.

3. The idea in a pure capitalist system is for the government to take a laissez-faire _____ toward business.

4. Because the costs of _____ the environment can affect all members of society, the government uses various legal means to try to protect the environment and make companies _____ with certain government regulations.

5. You may remember the BP oil _____ in the Gulf of Mexico in 2010, which resulted in the worst environmental _____ in U.S. history.

6. The company was charged with _____ safety and environmental regulations in building and managing the well that spilled the oil.

7. The government intervenes to see that businesses remain _____; antitrust laws were passed to prevent companies from joining together to unfairly control prices, what we call price-_____.

8. The second method government uses to maintain _____ in the economy is _____, the money that the government spends.

9. The government can raise taxes to take money out of the economy and lower the _____ rate.

10. When the president and Congress do not work together, or when the two parties do not work together, a political _____ can occur.

B **Check the spelling of the vocabulary words with your teacher. Discuss the meanings of these words and any other unfamiliar words in the sentences.**

PREDICTIONS

Think about the questions in the Topic Preview on page 122 and the sentences you heard in the Vocabulary Preview. Write three questions that you think will be answered in the lecture. Share your questions with your classmates.

NOTETAKING PREPARATION

Preparing for the Lecture by Reading

Most U.S. college and university teachers plan their lectures assuming that students will have read assigned chapters before class.

A lecture will usually deal with points in the assigned text, so you will be better prepared for the lecture by doing the reading ahead of time. When you read to prepare for a lecture, you may want to take reading notes. A good reader-notetaker needs to decide which points are main ones and which are details. If you take reading notes, you should use abbreviations and key words for efficiency and use indentation for better organization and clarity.

A Read the following text carefully.

The Role of Government

1 Americans have been debating the role of the federal government ever since the American Revolution in the 1770s. The 13 original colonies, which banded together to declare their independence from Britain, were very suspicious of a strong central government and protective of their individual rights as states. The Confederation government they formed saw the 13 original colonies through the Revolution.

2 A few years after the end of the Revolutionary War, though, the Confederation was unable to solve many problems facing the new nation, and the need for a stronger central government led to a new Constitution, which expanded the power of the national government. Still, the debate about the role of government went on in many areas, including the economic sphere. Thomas Jefferson, the third U.S. president, was a believer in laissez-faire economics; that is, he believed the government should not interfere in the economy. His general philosophy was "Government that governs least, governs best."

3 By today's standards, the role of the national, or federal, government in the economy was very small, consisting largely of setting tariffs and excise taxes as well as issuing currency. It wasn't until the time of the Civil War in the 1860s that the first income tax was instituted. Before that time, the government did not have money for internal improvements to the country.

4 After that time, the government began to expand its role in the economy. The Industrial Revolution, which was occurring at the same time, led to demands for the government to expand its role in the regulation of railroads and other big business. During these years, the government tended to support big business rather than organized labor. During the early years of the twentieth century, the government began to debate its role in the economy more sharply. President Theodore Roosevelt and President Woodrow Wilson took steps toward controlling the excessive power of big business.

5 However, it was the Great Depression of the 1930s that led most people to give up the idea of a laissez-faire economy. President Franklin Roosevelt led the

government to take an increased role in the welfare of the people. His New Deal instituted programs by which the government provided employment for large numbers of unemployed people and provided support through welfare for others. His administration also instituted the Social Security system, by which workers pay into a fund that then provides a kind of insurance protection for older, retired workers and disabled workers. In the years following the New Deal, the role of the government in the economy continued to expand. During the 1960s there emerged a new conservative viewpoint, and efforts were made by many in politics to loosen the control of the government on the economy and to return to a more laissez-faire economy. This issue is still being debated.

B **For questions 1 and 2, circle the correct answer. For questions 3, 4, and 5, write short answers.**

1. In general, has the role of the federal government become

   a. stronger   b. weaker   c. varied in degree   d. stayed the same over the years?

2. Which paragraph 2 notes seem most accurate?
   a. Cent govt = weaker — P. Jefferson agreed
   b. Cent govt = stronger — P. Jefferson opposed
   c. Cent govt = stronger b/c of laissez-faire

3. What details in paragraph 3 support the main idea of the paragraph?

   _____

4. Write a note for the main idea of paragraph 4, in your own words.

   _____

5. What details in paragraph 5 support the idea that government expanded in the 1930s?

   _____

C **Discourse Cues** **Number the following excerpts from the lecture from 1 to 5 in the order that you think you will probably hear them. Discuss with a partner or as a class the discourse cues that helped you figure out the order.**

_____ Let me begin today by saying that the American economy is basically a capitalist economy.

_____ So, these three methods—taxation, expenditure, and setting the interest rate—are the government's main means of maintaining the economy's stability.

_____ An important reason that the government tries to regulate the economy is to protect the environment.

_____ Another reason the government intervenes in the economy is to help people who for some reason beyond their control earn little or no income.

_____ The last reason for the government's intervention in the economy is to maintain economic stability.

FIRST LISTENING

CD 5, TR 2

(A) Listen to the beginning of the lecture. Circle the set of notes below that best records the information you hear.

a.

```
I. Am econ = cap. econ
   A. Am cap — indiv own prop
      1. house, land, business, intel prop (song/
         poem/bk/inven)
   B. free ent = make/buy/sell goods & lab
   C. free, compet markets
      1. bus suc, stay market; bus fail, leave
   D. not ev/o find job; not all bus sec
   E. gov does not intf in eco
II. Pure cap syst
   A. l-f att = limtd gov role
      1. nat def
      2. laws protect own & use prv prop
      3. prov wh bus doesn't, ex. rds
   B. US not pure cap econ or comp l-f att
      1. govt role bus ↑ 20th c, esp. 1930s
      2. US expanded role compli
Discuss 4 reasons govt intervenes
```

b.

```
Cap. econ
   • indiv own prop
   • intell prop =song, poem, etc.
   • free prod/buy/sell gds
   • bus succd, sty; fail, lve
I. Pure captlst econ
   • natl def
   • laws protct prv prop
   • bld rds, schls (bus won't provd)
II. US not cap syst
   • US not LF att to bus
   • gov role in bus 20th C↑
      1. start 1930s
   • issues today
```

CD 5, TR 3

(B) Now listen to the whole lecture and take notes. Look at the lecturer's visual aids as you listen. These may help you understand parts of the lecture.

Subtopic 1: Protecting the Environment

Protecting the Environment

- Regulations
  - Pollution control equipment
  - Disposal of toxic waste
- BP oil spill

Subtopic 2: <u>Helping People</u>

> **Public Assistance Programs/ Welfare**
> - Children
> - The elderly
> - The ill/disabled
> - The unemployed

Subtopic 3: <u>Protecting Competition</u>

> **Protecting Competition**
> - Antitrust laws
> - Monopoly regulation
> - Financial crisis of 2008

Subtopic 4: _Maintaining Economic Stability_

> **Maintaining Economic Stability**
>
> - Taxation
> - Government expenditures
> - Control of interest rates

SECOND LISTENING

Listen to the lecture again and make your notes as complete as possible.

THIRD LISTENING

A You will hear part of the lecture again. Listen and complete the notes by adding the information from the box.

↑	→	↓	BUT	condtns	Expend	indus	"

Stabilizing Econ
  A. Taxes
    1. econ grow too fast _____ inflat, so . . .
    2. gov't _____ taxes — take $ out of econ & _____ inflat
    3. _____ danger of unemploy, so . . .
    4. govt uses taxes to bal unemploy & inflat
  B. _____
    1. govt — huge amnt of $
    2. how to spend $ dep on econ _____ in
      a. diff _____
      b. _____ parts of cntry

B Compare your answers with a partner. Then compare the notes in **A** with the notes you took for this part of the lecture.

ACCURACY CHECK

CD 5, TR 6

A Listen to the following questions and write short answers. Use your notes. You will hear each question one time only.

1. _____
2. _____
3. _____
4. _____
5. _____
6. _____
7. _____
8. _____
9. _____
10. _____

B Check your answers with your teacher. If your score is less than 70 percent, you may need to listen to the lecture again and rewrite some of your notes.

ORAL SUMMARY

Use your notes to create an oral summary of the lecture with your partner. As you work together, add details to your notes that your partner included but you had missed.

DISCUSSION

Discuss the following questions with a classmate or in a small group.

1. Which of the four reasons for government intervention in the economy makes the most sense to you? Why?

2. What are the advantages of a laissez-faire economy? What are the disadvantages?

3. If a government has to decide between creating jobs in mining and industry and protecting the environment, which should they choose? Explain.

4. Should government provide welfare support to people who are unable to support themselves, or is this the responsibility of the family? Explain.

PRE-READING

The following Reading is about the Himalayan nation of Bhutan. Before you read, answer the following questions. Share your answers with a classmate.

1. Scan the article. What kind of government did Bhutan have in the past? What kind of government does it have now?

2. Based on what you learned in the lecture, do you expect that the government of Bhutan will play a larger or smaller role in the country's economy under the new type of government than it did under the old type of government? Why?

READING

Now read the article.

Bhutan's Enlightened Experiment

Bhutan is a country that is attempting the impossible: to jump from the Middle Ages to the twenty-first century without losing its balance.

For more than a thousand years, this tiny country has survived in magnificent isolation, a place the size of Switzerland set between two giants, India and China. Closed off from the outside world both by geography and deliberate policy, the country had no roads, no electricity, no motor vehicles, no telephones, no postal service until the 1960s. It looks like a place that time forgot: ancient temples high on cliffs; unclimbed mountain peaks rising above unpolluted rivers and forests.

But not everything was perfect in Bhutan. When King Jigme Singye Wangchuck became king in 1972,

Bhutan had some of the highest poverty, illiteracy, and infant-mortality rates in the world—a result of the policy of isolation. His father, Bhutan's third king, had begun opening up the country in the 1960s, building roads, establishing schools and health clinics, pushing for United Nations membership. King Jigme Singye Wangchuck would go much further. He has tried to control Bhutan's opening to the world—and in the process redefine the very meaning of development. The phrase he invented to describe his approach: Gross National Happiness.

Guided by the "four pillars of Gross National Happiness"—sustainable development, environmental protection, cultural preservation, and good governance—Bhutan has pulled itself out of terrible poverty without harming its natural resources. Nearly three-quarters of the country is still covered by forests, with more than 25 percent protected from development—among the highest percentages in the world. Rates of illiteracy and infant mortality have fallen dramatically, and the economy is booming. Tourism is growing, too. In 1999, Bhutan granted its citizens access to television—the last country on the planet to do so.

Now comes the most important step in Bhutan's experiment: the move to democracy. In 2006, King Jigme Singye Wangchuck decided to give up his throne to give power to the people, setting up a series of events for the year 2008 that ended in the formation of the country's first democratic government.

The real test of Gross National Happiness, then, has just begun. Bhutan's new leaders will face many challenges. One challenge is that the citizens loved their king and are suspicious of democracy. The outside world is watching closely, wondering if this tiny Himalayan nation might help answer some of humankind's most difficult questions: How can a society maintain its identity in the face of globalization? How can it take advantage of the good of the modern world without being overwhelmed by the bad? And can there ever be a happy balance between tradition and development?

To survive in democratic politics, Bhutan's new government will have to make the people happy. As the country modernizes, that may depend on relations with the outside world. As of 2008, Bhutan had established connections with only 21 countries; the most important is India, which provides military security and buys 80 percent of Bhutan's exports. Most big powers, including the United States, aren't on the list, because Bhutan worries about being controlled by others. However, Bhutan is moving toward membership in the World Trade Organization (WTO). In a globalized economy, no country can fully protect itself from trade—and, therefore, the WTO. "Our greatest fear," government minister Jigme Y. Thinley said, "comes from the unknown."

DISCUSSION

Discuss these questions with a classmate.

1. Does the economy of Bhutan fit the definition of a capitalist economy given in the lecture? Explain your answer.

2. Which of the reasons for regulating the economy mentioned in the lecture were also mentioned in the Reading? Compare examples about the United States to examples about Bhutan.

3. What are some of the advantages that a monarchy has over a democracy when it comes to making widespread, rapid changes to a country's economy?

PURSUING THE TOPIC

Explore the topic of this chapter further by doing the following.

Individually or with a partner, choose one of the issues mentioned in the lecture and research the positions of the two major political parties in the United States, the Democrats or the Republicans. Take notes and prepare a short presentation comparing and contrasting their views on the issue.

www.ontheissues.org/democratic_party.htm
www.ontheissues.org/republican_party.htm

TOPIC PREVIEW

Discuss the following questions with a partner or your classmates.

1. What are the benefits of a written constitution, a document that the government must follow? What disadvantages might there be?

2. In your culture, where do the laws come from? Can a law change over time, that is, can it ever be seen as illegal?

3. Should branches of government—for example, the executive, legislative, and judicial branches—have equal power? Explain.

Tourists view historical U.S. documents at the National Archives, Washington, DC.

VOCABULARY PREVIEW

CD 5, TR 7

A **Read through the sentences below, which are missing vocabulary from the lecture. As you read, try to imagine which words would fit in the blanks. Then listen to the sentences and write the missing words in the blanks.**

1. Before we begin our discussion of the two important _____ of the U.S. government, let's take a look at the three _____ that make up the U.S. government.

2. The Congress is primarily responsible for _____, or making, new laws that are to be followed by the 50 states of the country.

3. The executive branch _____ the laws that _____ in the legislature.

4. After the president has signed a new law, the executive branch of the government is responsible for seeing that the new law is _____, or carried out.

5. The judicial branch decides any kind of legal issue that falls under federal _____.

6. A president who feels very strongly that a new law is wrong may refuse to sign it. Congress can _____ a presidential _____, but it is a very difficult thing to do.

7. If an investigation shows that illegal activities probably did take place, Congress has the power to _____, or charge, the person. This did not happen to President Nixon, who _____ before Congress could act.

8. The U.S. Supreme Court, the highest court in the judicial branch, hears cases involving the _____ of federal laws enacted by Congress.

9. In 2012, the Court heard arguments that challenged parts of a controversial health-care bill that was _____ passed by the legislature.

10. The president can check the power of the judicial branch because he is the person who _____ candidates to be federal judges, including those on the Supreme Court.

B **Check the spelling of the vocabulary words with your teacher. Discuss the meanings of these words and any other unfamiliar words in the sentences.**

PREDICTIONS

Think about the questions in the Topic Preview on page 132 and the sentences you heard in the Vocabulary Preview. Write three questions that you think will be answered in the lecture. Share your questions with your classmates.

NOTETAKING PREPARATION

Pre-Lecture Reading and Key Words

As mentioned in the previous chapter, U.S. university students most often prepare for each class with an assigned reading—a text chapter, an article, or even a case study. This preparation makes the instructor's lecture, which is usually on a topic related to the reading, easier to follow and to take notes on. You will notice how this pre-lecture reading will aid your comprehension of the lecture.

Using key words in your lecture notes allows you to take down important information quickly. You can also use key words to take notes on a reading. Think of the key words as notes on the reading that you can use to study in the future.

A Read the following passage carefully.

> ### Judicial Review
>
> Judicial review is the power of a court to invalidate, or overturn, any law passed by the legislature that the court believes to be unconstitutional. The concept of judicial review as exercised by the Supreme Court of the United States is almost unique in the world. It can be called an American invention. Nowhere else does the judiciary of a country exercise final say over laws passed by the legislature. This enormous power of judicial review by the Supreme Court was established in a famous case several years after the Constitution was written, *Marbury v. Madison* (1803). The Court stated that the Constitution was superior to any acts by the legislature and that it was the Court's duty to void any laws that went against the Constitution. This power was not explicitly expressed in the Constitution, and even today, almost 200 years later, the Supreme Court's power to void laws passed by the legislature is still controversial.
>
> If we compare judicial review in the United States with that in a few other countries, we will see just how unusual it is. In Great Britain, the right of Parliament (the legislature) to make any law it wants to make cannot be challenged by the courts. The courts can interpret a law but not decide if a law is valid. In Germany, the judiciary has had the power of judicial review since shortly after World War II, but it has been slow to exercise judicial review for cultural and historical reasons. The judiciary in Canada has had this judicial review power since 1982.

B Write answers to the following comprehension questions using key words.

1. What is judicial review?

_____

2. Is judicial review guaranteed by the U.S. Constitution? Explain.

_____

3. Which of the following countries has no provisions for judicial review—Britain, Canada, or Germany?

_____

4. Do Germany and Canada exercise judicial review more or less frequently than the United States does? Explain.

_____

C Study the chart below and answer the two questions that follow. The chart shows some of the powers of each branch of the U.S. government and how some of these powers may be limited by the other two branches.

The U.S. Government		
Executive Branch	**Legislative Branch**	**Judicial Branch**
• Proposes new legislation to Congress • May veto bills passed by Congress • Nominates judges • Makes treaties with other countries • Prepares federal budget	• Approves federal budget • Approves treaties • Sends bills it has passed to president for signature • May override a president's veto by a two-thirds majority • Must approve appointment of judges • May impeach the president	• Interprets laws • May declare a law unconstitutional • Interprets treaties

1. Which powers in each branch are checked by another branch?

_____

2. Which powers seem to have no checks against them?

_____

D **Discourse Cues** Number the following excerpts from the lecture from 1 to 5 in the order that you think you will probably hear them. Discuss with a partner or as a class the discourse cues that helped you figure out the order.

_____ In addition to separation of powers, a system of checks and balances was written into the Constitution.

_____ You might wonder what check the executive or the legislative branch has on the judicial branch.

_____ To start, the Constitution provides for three branches of government: one, the legislative; two, the executive; and three, the judicial.

_____ First, let's consider how the executive branch can check the power of the legislative branch.

_____ Knowing the three branches, you'll already have an idea of what is meant by _separation of powers_.

FIRST LISTENING

CD 5, TR 8

A Listen to the beginning of the lecture. Circle the set of notes below that best records the information you hear.

a.

US Constitution
- >225 yrs basis for stable govt
- basically unchanged
- oldest written const
Look @ 2 imp principals
- (1) Sep of powers
- (2) Sys of cks and bal
- 1st—3 branches of gov't

b.

US Constitution
- >225 yrs basis for stable govt
- basically unchanged
- US young cntry, but oldest written const
I. 2 imp princpls in Const
  A. 1 Sep of powers and 2 sys cks and bal
II. 3 branches of gov't

c.

US Constitution
1987=200th anniv
basically unchanged
US oldest const in wrld
A. 2 imp prncpls in Const
B. 3 branches of gov'

CD 5, TR 9

B Now listen to the whole lecture and take notes. Look at the lecturer's visual aids as you listen. These may help you understand parts of the lecture.

Subtopic 1: _____

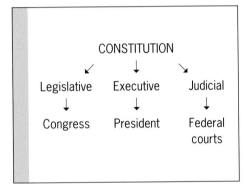

Subtopic 2: _____

Constitution
- Each branch has its own power
- No single branch can have all the power
- Checks and balances prevent abuse of power

Subtopic 3: _____

> Executive → Legislature
> Legislature → Executive
> Judiciary → Legislature
> Executive and Legislature → Judiciary

SECOND LISTENING

Listen to the lecture again and make your notes as complete as possible.

THIRD LISTENING

A You will hear part of the lecture again. Listen and complete the notes by adding the information from the box.

| apprvd | oppty | Jud | SC | ?ed | abt | sep | √ |

Exec & Leg Ck on _____
- Pres nom fed judgs, inc _____ (9 judgs)
  ○ _____ to chng bal of SC
- Senate apprvs Pres's nom = _____ on both Exec & Jud
  ○ Nom for SC _____ by Senate
    • e.g. ? _____ record & opinions: abortin, gun contrl, _____ of church & state, etc.
  ○ Most nom _____, but not all

B Compare your answers with a partner. Then compare the notes in **A** with the notes you took for this part of the lecture.

ACCURACY CHECK

CD 5, TR 12

A Listen to the following questions and write short answers. Use your notes. You will hear each question one time only.

1. _____
2. _____
3. _____
4. _____
5. _____
6. _____
7. _____
8. _____
9. _____
10. _____

B Check your answers with your teacher. If your score is less than 70 percent, you may need to listen to the lecture again and rewrite some of your notes.

ORAL SUMMARY

Use your notes to create an oral summary of the lecture with your partner. As you work together, add details to your notes that your partner included but you had missed.

DISCUSSION

Discuss the following questions with a classmate or in a small group.

1. Do the two principles of (1) separation of powers and (2) checks and balances make the United States easier or more difficult to govern? Why?

2. How is the power to make and enforce laws in your culture divided? Explain.

3. Can a law be overturned by the courts or another branch of government in your culture?

4. Do you think a branch of government should have the power to remove a president from office? Explain.

PRE-READING

The following Reading is about the government of ancient Rome. Before you read, answer the following questions. Share your answers with a classmate.

1. Why do people continue to study ancient Roman civilization? What contributions did the ancient Romans make to the world?

2. What type of government did the ancient Romans have? Discuss what you know about the executive, legislative, and judicial functions of ancient Roman government.

READING

Now read the article.

The World According to Rome

Fifteen centuries after the fall of Rome, the influence of the Roman Empire—in language, literature, legal codes, government, architecture, medicine, sports, arts, engineering, etc.—can still be felt in the daily lives of people all over the world. One Roman ideal in particular has had a large impact on American government: that of the written law used to protect individuals against one another and against the power of the state. In fact, the Romans took this practice from the Greeks, but it was Rome that put this abstract idea into daily practice. A Latin inscription at Harvard Law School expresses the idea very clearly: *Non sub homine sed sub deo et lege*—It is not by men but by God and the law we are governed.

In the ongoing struggle between the ordinary people of Rome and those in power, the ordinary people, called the *plebeians*, or *plebs*, decided they would much rather rely on laws than their all-too-human rulers. Under pressure from the plebs, the governing class was repeatedly forced to issue written codes. In 450 BC, the first of these documents, the Twelve Tables, came out, and the Romans continued to publish legal codes for the next thousand years. A collection of these codes, completed by the emperor Justinian in AD 534, has served as the foundation of Western law ever since.

The ancient Roman process of making laws also had a deep influence on the American system. During the era of the Roman Republic (509 to 49 BC), lawmaking involved two houses of government, just as it does in the United States today. Legislation was first passed by the *comitia*, the assembly of citizens, then approved by the members of the upper class, the senate, and finally issued in the name of the senate and the people of Rome.

Centuries later, when the American Founding Fathers began their bold experiment in democratic government, they took republican Rome as their model. American laws must also be approved by two legislative bodies. The House of Representatives is similar to the Roman assembly of citizens. The U.S. Senate, like the Roman senate, was originally established as a body of members of the social and political elite. (It was not until the Seventeenth Amendment to the Constitution was passed that ordinary American citizens were allowed to vote for their senators.) Impressed by the checks and balances of the Roman system, the authors of the American Constitution made sure that an official could be "impeached," or removed from office. The word *impeached* is a word that is taken from the Latin *in pedica*.

This genuine respect for the power of law was reflected in the behavior of the otherwise all-powerful Roman emperors, who for the most part felt obligated to obey these written codes. And if the emperor himself had to honor the law, the obligation fell even more heavily on lower-ranking officials and colonial governors. Any official who violated the law could be called back to Rome, where he would be put *in pedica*, into chains. In fact, the establishment in the United States Constitution of an independent judicial branch with judges and juries has its roots in these ancient Roman legal practices.

DISCUSSION

Discuss these questions with a classmate.

1. What similarities and differences are there between the executive power of the emperor in ancient Rome, and the executive branch of the U.S. government?

2. What similarities and differences are there between the legislature in ancient Rome, and the legislative branch of the U.S. government?

3. How did ancient Roman ideals affect the development of the judicial system of the United States?

PURSUING THE TOPIC

Explore the topic of this chapter further by doing the following.

Watch the movie *All the President's Men*, a movie about President Richard Nixon, who resigned before being impeached for an abuse of presidential power. Be prepared to discuss the movie with your classmates.

CHAPTER 15

Common Law and the Jury System

TOPIC PREVIEW

Discuss the following questions with a partner or your classmates.

1. If you were accused of a crime and went to court, who would you prefer to decide if you were innocent or guilty, a judge or a group of your peers on a jury?

2. Do you think of laws as something written and unchangeable? Or can laws change over time according to changes in a culture?

3. Should criminals receive lighter sentences for their crimes for cooperating with the police, for example, by telling them about another person who did something illegal?

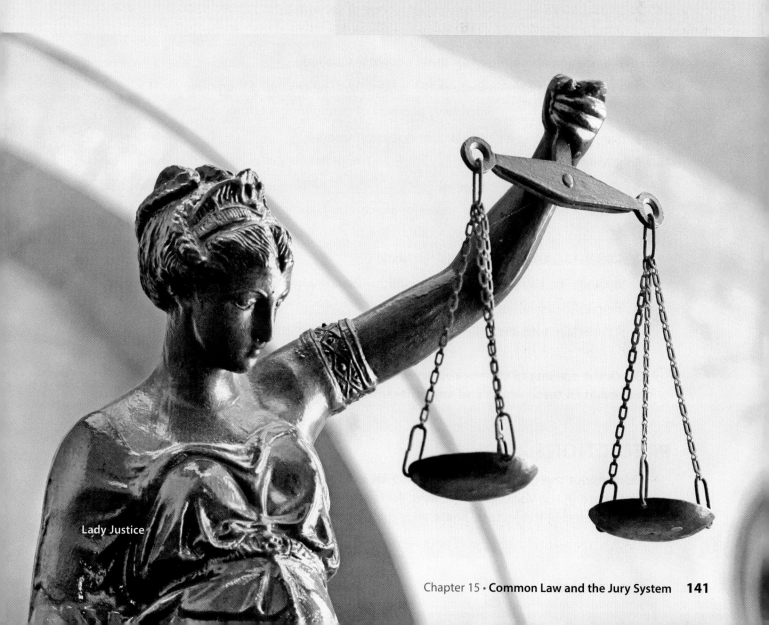

Lady Justice

VOCABULARY PREVIEW

CD 5, TR 13

A **Read through the sentences below, which are missing vocabulary from the lecture. As you read, try to imagine which words would fit in the blanks. Then listen to the sentences and write the missing words in the blanks.**

1. The basic principle of the U.S. legal system is that an accused person is _____ until proven _____.

2. In deciding a case, under _____ law, the judge consults a _____, a complex set of written laws.

3. The judge also decides what _____ the defendant, that is, the person accused of wrongdoing, will be given if guilty.

4. To determine the defendant's guilt under common law, the judge also considers the _____ set by other court decisions.

5. Very often, it is not the judge who gives a _____, but the jury, a group of six or twelve ordinary citizens, who decide the defendant's guilt or innocence and, in civil cases, how much money should be paid in _____.

6. In either civil or criminal trials, the jury hears _____ from people with information about the case; these people are called _____.

7. Criminal trials are ones where the government, representing the public, _____ individuals accused of committing a crime.

8. The defendant in a criminal case does not have to _____; it is the government's job to _____ the person is guilty.

9. The reason that the degree of _____ is much higher in a criminal trial is that a person's freedom and even life can be taken away if he or she is _____, that is, found guilty, of a crime.

10. Michael Jackson's doctor was convicted of _____ manslaughter, meaning he caused his patient's death without intending to.

11. Often the defendant is allowed to _____ bargain only if he or she also cooperates with the _____ in bringing other criminals to justice.

B **Check the spelling of the vocabulary words with your teacher. Discuss the meanings of these words and any other unfamiliar words in the sentences.**

PREDICTIONS

Think about the questions in the Topic Preview on page 141 and the sentences you heard in the Vocabulary Preview. Write three questions that you think will be answered in the lecture. Share your questions with your classmates.

NOTETAKING PREPARATION

Pre-Lecture Reading and Abbreviations and Symbols

As mentioned in previous chapters, U.S. university students are expected to arrive in class with some background on the topic that the professor will lecture on or that students will be asked to apply to questions or problems posed by the professor in class. Doing the reading will help you put the parts of the lecture together in your mind.

Besides preparing you for class, the notes you take on the reading will give you an efficient record of what you've read. Using abbreviations and symbols and organizing the information on the page will make it easier to review the notes before class or before a quiz.

A Read the following passage carefully.

Jury Selection

Serving on a jury in the United States to determine the guilt or innocence of an accused person is one of the most important civic duties a citizen can perform. Jurors are randomly selected from voter registration—and sometimes drivers' license—lists. To serve on a jury, a person must be a U.S. citizen, be at least 18 years old, live in the judicial district for a year, and know English well enough to follow the court proceedings. People with a serious mental or physical condition or with a felony record are disqualified from serving on a jury. Members of the military on active duty, police and firefighters, as well as public officials may not serve on federal juries. Also, people for whom jury duty would cause a severe hardship or inconvenience are often excused. Employers by law cannot penalize an employee for missing work to serve on a jury, but someone who lost wages to serve on a jury would be under a hardship to serve. Potential jurors fill out questionnaires to see if they are qualified to serve. These methods help to ensure that jurors represent a cross section of the community without consideration of race, gender, national origin, age, or political affiliation.

Being called for jury duty does not mean a person will actually serve. The judge and lawyers involved in an actual case have the opportunity to question potential jurors in order to exclude those who may not be able to decide the case fairly. Potential jurors who know someone in the case, who have information about the case, or who may have strong prejudices about the case will typically be excused by the judge. The lawyers for the defense and the prosecution may also exclude a certain number of jurors without giving a reason. A person who is against the death sentence would probably be excluded by the judge in a capital case, in other words, a case that could call for the death penalty if the defendant were found guilty. This is a clear-cut example. Lawyers defending or prosecuting a defendant will often have far less obvious reasons for excluding a potential jury member.

B Write answers to the following comprehension questions using abbreviations and symbols. Write headings to the left and details under the heading to the right, as shown under question 1.

1. What four criteria must a person in the U.S. meet to serve on a jury?

      1. *4 criteria to be a U.S. juror*

          a. _____

          b. _____

          c. _____

          d. _____

2. Who is disqualified from serving on a jury?

3. Which potential jurors are excluded as being unable to decide a case fairly?

C **Discourse Cues** Number the following excerpts from the lecture from 1 to 5 in the order that you think you will probably hear them. Discuss with a partner or as a class the discourse cues that helped you figure out the order.

_____ Although different from many legal systems, the U.S. system of justice is not unique.

_____ To start out today, let me say that the legal system of a country—that is, its system of justice—reflects the history and culture of the country just as much as the other topics we have discussed so far.

_____ I don't want to leave you with the impression that every legal case is tried in court with a jury in the United States.

_____ Now that you've had a chance to think about these philosophical questions, let's begin by looking at the U.S. legal system in terms of what makes it different from legal systems in many other countries.

_____ Now I'd like to discuss two other big differences, namely between criminal and civil trials.

FIRST LISTENING

Listen to the lecture and take notes. Look at the lecturer's visual aids as you listen. These may help you understand parts of the lecture.

Introduction

> **Common Law and the Jury System**
>
> Introduction
> 1. Common law vs civil law
> 2. Jury system
> 3. Plea bargaining

Subtopic 1: _____

> **Civil Law**
> - Code of laws
> - Judge
>
> **Common Law**
> - Case by case
> - Judge
> - Jury

Subtopic 2: _____

> **The Jury System**
> - Civil trials
> - Criminal trials
> - Judge vs. jury
> - Criticisms

Subtopic 3: _____

> **Plea Bargaining/Settlements**
> - Criminal cases
> - Civil cases

🔊 SECOND LISTENING
CD 5, TR 15

Listen to the lecture again and make your notes as complete as possible.

THIRD LISTENING

CD 5, TR 16

A You will hear part of the lecture again. Listen and complete the notes by adding the information from the box.

| bet | citz | def | not | Rt | vs. | $ | ++ |

_____ to trial by jury guarntd by US Const

Jury = 6 or 12 ordin _____ ; hear testmny in civil or crim trials & reach verdct

I. Civil trial: disp _____ prvt ind re: contrcts, prop. rts
   A. jury decd who wins—which side > evidnce?
   B. _____ must testify
   C. jury decd _____ to winner

II. Crim trial: gov't _____ accusd of crim
   A. jury decd guilt or innoc—"beyond a reason. doubt"
   B. gov't must prv guilt—_____ def prv innoc
   C. def doesn't have to testify
   D. deg of proof _____ bec if convctd, crim's free or life taken away

B Compare your answers with a partner. Then compare the notes in **A** with the notes you took for this part of the lecture.

ACCURACY CHECK

CD 5, TR 17

A **Listen to the following questions and write short answers. Use your notes. You will hear each question one time only.**

1. _____

2. _____

3. _____

4. _____

5. _____

6. _____

7. _____

8. _____

9. _____

10. _____

B **Check your answers with your teacher. If your score is less than 70 percent, you may need to listen to the lecture again and rewrite some of your notes.**

ORAL SUMMARY

Use your notes to create an oral summary of the lecture with your partner. As you work together, add details to your notes that your partner included but you had missed.

DISCUSSION

Discuss the following questions with a classmate or in a small group.

1. Which principle of law do you think is fairer, "innocent until proven guilty" or "guilty until proven innocent"? Why?

2. Compare the advantages of having a judge decide a case without a jury to the advantages of having a jury decide a case.

3. In plea bargaining, is it fair to the victim of a crime if the guilty person receives a less severe punishment for cooperating with the state? Explain.

PRE-READING

The following Reading is about the countries that are beginning to use juries in their legal system. Before you read, answer the following questions. Share your answers with a classmate.

1. Are juries used in your country of origin? If so, how are they used? Are you aware of any countries other than the United States that use a jury system?

2. Look at the title. Why do you think a country would want to try using juries as a part of its legal system?

READING

Now read the article.

Experimenting with the Jury System

When you hear the word *jury*, what image comes to mind? Most likely, you will picture an American courtroom drama as seen in countless movies and television programs. It is indeed true that the jury system is an essential part of the U.S. legal system; a majority of both civil and criminal cases in the United States every year are heard by a jury. It is perhaps less well-known that a number of other countries in the world also use juries in their legal systems. In fact, despite criticisms of the U.S. jury system, more and more countries around the world are beginning to experiment with the use of juries.

In 2009, Japan reinstated the jury system, after having abandoned it in 1943. The jury system in

Japan is far more limited than in the United States, however. Juries are used only in criminal cases involving serious crimes such as murder and rape. In such cases, six citizen jurors randomly chosen from among those registered to vote serve alongside three professional judges. The jurors must be at least 20 years old and have at least a junior high school education. In order to find a defendant guilty, at least one of the professional judges must agree with all six of the citizen jurors. On the other hand, a not-guilty verdict by at least five of the jurors will stand, even if all three of the professional judges vote for a guilty verdict.

South Korea has also recently begun to use juries. Starting in 2008, the country began a five-year experiment using American-style jury trials. South Korean juries have five to nine members. During this experimental period, the decision of the jury is considered advisory; that is, the judge does not have to follow the jury's decision. At the end of the experimental period, the South Korean Supreme Court will decide which, if any, aspects of the new system will be permanently adopted.

In Hunan Province in China, home to some 100 million citizens, the use of a "people's jury" has been in place since 2007. Jurors are randomly chosen from a large pool of people who are selected by local officials. Usually, but not always, the pool consists of people who live in the town or city where the crime was committed. Typically seven to nine (but sometimes as many as thirteen) people are randomly chosen from the pool to sit on the jury. These jurors attend the court proceedings. At the end, they give their opinions on both the facts and an appropriate sentence. They are not required to reach a unanimous decision, and as in South Korea, their decisions are merely advisory. The people's jury is typically used in criminal cases involving what are considered to be sensitive or difficult matters that have the potential to affect group harmony or stability. They often involve cases that could result in the death penalty.

As you can see, there are many differences in the ways juries function in the U.S., Japan, South Korea, and China. However, one common theme seems to be a belief that at least in theory, ordinary citizens have an important role to play in the judicial process.

DISCUSSION

Discuss these questions with a classmate.

1. What are the differences between the jury system in the United States and the new jury system in Japan?

2. What are the differences between the way juries are used in South Korea and China and the jury system in the United States?

3. Considering the criticisms that are made of the jury system in the U.S., why do you think some countries are starting to use juries in a limited way?

PURSUING THE TOPIC

Explore the topic of this chapter further by doing the following.

Watch the movie *12 Angry Men*, either the original 1957 version or the 1997 HBO remake. This drama is about a jury deciding a murder case. Be prepared to discuss the movie with your classmates.

Demon Fish

TOPIC PREVIEW

Read the situation below. Then discuss with a partner what *a representative of the hotel industry*, *a local politician*, and *a tourist* in the town would want to see happen.

A small beach town on the U.S. Atlantic coast depends on tourism as its main industry. It is tourist season and a shark has been seen swimming near the beach for two days.

VOCABULARY PREVIEW

A **Read the definitions of these key words and phrases that you will hear during the video.**

a natural transition a reasonable or normal change from one thing to another
time and time again over and over again; repeatedly
abstract threat a danger that exists in one's mind rather than based on a real event
familiar with knowing someone or something fairly well
within a span of during the period of time of
stamp out remove; put an end to something
halt stop something or someone
hold politicians accountable for force politicians to take responsibility for something
political penalty the consequence for a politician of an unpopular decision or bad behavior

B **Work with a partner and write vocabulary from A in the blanks in the sentences.**

1. The _____ for voting against the president was losing reelection.

2. There were four shark attacks _____ twelve days, but the local politicians did nothing to try to _____ them.

3. Are you _____ the movie *Jaws*, which is about a shark attack?

4. This is not a(n) _____. People are dying and something must be done.

5. The police are trying hard to _____ drug dealing in the area.

6. _____ voters want to _____ events that they really cannot control.

7. When the senator lost the election, she made _____ from politics to business.

VIEWING

🖵 FIRST VIEWING

Watch the video, and then compare your first impressions with a partner. Talk about what you remember, what surprised you, and what interested you.

🖵 SECOND VIEWING

Watch the video again. Listen for the missing words and write them in the blanks.

1. I've spent the vast majority of my reporting career here in _____ covering politicians.

2. The first recorded shark _____ in history in the late 1500s comes from a Portuguese sailor who had the misfortune to _____ overboard.

3. This in some ways was the inspiration for the _____ *Jaws*.

4. In fact, Woodrow Wilson, who was _____ at the time and started his political career in New Jersey, actually came under attack for the fact that he did _____ to halt these shark strikes.

President Woodrow Wilson

5. And so it was just interesting to see how voters really did _____ Woodrow Wilson and thought that, you know, there was something he could do to ensure that they could be _____ at sea.

Complete these notes as you watch the video. Write only important words, not full sentences, and abbreviate common words.

1) Early sh. attks
    – late 1500s _____
    – many tales _____
    – capts _____

2) Abst. threat – but changed
    – beachgoers _____
    – front pg Phil. Inq. _____
    – ppl more aware, but _____

3) Then 4 ppl _____ in 12 _____
    – Woodrow Wilson, pres: _____
    – voters _____ WW

AFTER VIEWING

ORAL SUMMARY

Use your notes to create an oral summary of the video with your partner. As you work together, add details to your notes that your partner included but you had missed.

DISCUSSION

Discuss the following questions with a classmate or in a small group.

1. The speaker says jokingly, "Many people said it was obviously a natural transition from politicians to sharks." Why is this funny?

2. Why did Woodrow Wilson lose some votes during his election?

3. What can the government do to make beaches safe places in many different ways, not just from the threat of sharks?

Videoscripts

Cowboys in North America

Thank you for having me here tonight and thank all of you for coming. The cowboy basically breaks into four different types: the *vaquero*, which is the traditional roots of the cowboy in North America; and then the *buckaroo* region, which is west of the Rockies; *cowboys* are kind of east of the Rockies; and *cow punchers* are Arizona, New Mexico, Oklahoma, Texas.

You know, I find it amazing I guess in the U.S., that you know, here we live in one of the most high-tech, richest countries in the world, and these people have been able to hold on to their culture, because they love the lifestyle. I mean, a lot of these guys have done other jobs or tried other jobs. Merlin told me that—I asked him if he'd ever worked as anything other than a cowboy and he said yeah, he'd worked at the railroad for one day and he quit; and he worked at a goldmine for one day and he quit.

So, you know, a typical single guy at one of these ranches makes anywhere from eight to twelve hundred dollars a month. They get housing and three meals a day. But they're working seventy to a hundred hours a week. So, when you do the math on it, it's, you know, three to four dollars an hour. And you better love what you're doing. But I find it amazing that there are some cultures that really almost disappear within one or two generations when they're exposed to progress or so-called progress. And these people have for a hundred and fifty years basically continued to do what they've done.

A lot of the gear they use hasn't changed. I mean, what it takes to cowboy is good horse skills, skill with a rope, and a real understanding on how to work cattle on a horse. And you can tell that these guys love the outdoors, I mean, and love being by themselves, love working in these environments even though, you know, some of these guys, uh, Ronnie told me that in the winter, sometimes they've worked when it's fifty below, you know, ten hours, on a horse, fifty below. And you know, he says, it's cold, but you can live in it.

And you don't see a lot of women working as cowboys, and they don't mind being described as cowboys; it's kind of a working title of what they do. You know, generally you see young girls, women that are past child-bearing age because, you know, family's like the most central thing in these people's lives. I mean, that's everything to them.

This is a father and son up in Oregon. And these kids, I mean, kids are very impressive on these ranches, I mean, they give them, the kids have a lot of duties on a ranch, a working ranch. And kids get to see the full life cycle of, you know, spring, summer, fall, and winter.

Since the fencing in of the ranges back in the 1890s, everybody has predicted—called the cowboys, you know, a vanishing breed, last of a breed, dying breed. And I think it's really an evolving breed. It's a business, ranching's a business like any other business, and businesses that are determined to survive evolve, and so they found efficiencies. But still, the cheapest way to raise cattle is by feeding them grass, and you're not going to do that on a four-wheeler on 1.3 million acres. You're going to do it using guys like this. Thank you very much for coming.

Through the Eyes of a Critic

I brought some things from Galapagos as well. This is a trip where I couldn't bring family. I'm a married man. My wife's name is Monica. We work together to a large extent. We have two children—two boys, Aiden and Anskar, six and nine. On this trip, they couldn't come. And you miss them a lot, obviously. Most trips they can't come.

So, when I got back home, everybody was fast asleep. It was early, early morning. I just opened the door to our house. And I walked in. And I made myself a cup of coffee. And the dog greeted me, Douglas. Everybody else is asleep. And then I felt a little bit sorry for myself. It's like I'm missing out on so much. I see a lot. I experience a lot. But still, I miss maybe the most important thing, and that's my kids! You know.

So I was sitting there, drinking my coffee, you know, doing this with the dog. And then little Anskar, the oldest boy, came out, and he said, "Dad! You're home!" in his pajamas. And he hugged me, and he was sitting in my lap, and then said, "How was your assignment?"

I said, "Good, but never mind that. I'm home now darling. This is so good to see you. How are you?"

"Did you get any good pictures?"

And I said, "Yeah, well," I said.

"Can you show me?"

So I was sitting down with a computer showing him this land iguana with this Galapagos mockingbird, talking about this very interesting sort of collaborative effort, the bird rinsing parasites. The big lizard, that's a vegetarian, is actually walking through the vegetation, scaring up insects that the mockingbird can eat, etc. It's a nice symbiotic relationship. And he was like fascinated by this, Anskar.

And he said, "Well this is wonderful, Dad." And he was really interested. We looked at the sea lions, and we looked at all sorts of things. And he was he was sharing it, and it was so beautiful. It was like the best. You know the frigatebirds they can actually tell me when the orcas come out, come up to breathe because they will be, as you know, they're like scavengers, opportunists. And they will fly over the surface. And when there's a big predator, they will get very close. And they will hover. And the big orca will come up perhaps. And I told him about that, and he was like, "Wow!"

But when we came to this set of photographs, he, especially here, he said, "Dad," this little boy, "These are your best photographs ever."

And I said, "Well, gee, thanks."

And, "Yes, definitely," he said. "Definitely."

And I'm curious, you know, why, what this little boy, "Why do you think these pictures are better than any other pictures?"

And he said, "Well, don't you see? They're… the quality."

"Yeah, well, I do. I've done my best, you know. This is a marine iguana. And, yeah, I was sneaking up to it. And I was illuminating it with a soft box. And it took me ages because they're quite skittish and…"

"Ah, okay. Mmm." Well, but when we came to this picture, he's like, "This is it. This is the best."

And then I hugged him and said, "I love you, you know. Tell me why."

And he said, "Don't you understand?" (You know, like "*idiot*" you know, almost.) "But he's giving you a high five!"

UNIT 3 VIDEO

My Journey in the Muslim World

I was raised in a show-biz family in Manhattan and Malibu, California, and it was an exciting life full of cutting-edge artistic culture and a lot of freedom. So much more. And I left that life to be engaged in what's happening in the world and to travel far and deeply as a photojournalist.

This book is not meant to represent all Muslims everywhere. I'm not an expert on Islam. And it's just what I saw and experienced during my travels in these places. So here I hope to share a wider view of a group of people much misunderstood, especially since 9/11.

Now this is America. This is post 9/11, Muslim America. And it was a great time to kind of for me to revisit America. It was just a very, very classic immigrant experience, I think. I'm not Muslim, I'm not, you know, but they reminded me of my family. You know, a little bit of the old country, a lot of the new country, in this very rich American mix.

This is Dearborn, Michigan. And these are Ryazan dolls, and they're an alternative, Islamic alternative to Barbie.

And this lady fled the civil war in Lebanon. This is Dearborn. And you know Muslim Americans, like all Americans, have fled civil war, dictatorship, economic hardship. I mean, it's just like everybody else. But they were under a certain amount of pressure at that time. And *National Geographic* asked me to go out and see how they were doing and to describe their lives visually.

This is Latif Muhammad, and Florence Muhammad is reflected in the mirror with her granddaughter, Kelly. And they're in a place called New Medinah, Mississippi, which is near Sumrall and it's a Muslim, mostly Muslim village of farmers. And they're mainstream Sunni Muslims.

And this is Zulia Martinez. She is Mexican-American convert to Islam. More and more Hispanic-Americans are converting to Islam. This is in Houston. And this is at a baptism party for one of her Catholic relatives.

This is just the end of the day after a fair in Dearborn. Rainstorm.

And this is Graterford, Pennsylvania, and it's a maximum-security prison. There are about 3,200 prisoners here and 800 of them are Muslim. Most of them are African-American. Most of them are mainstream Muslims, and they were incredibly protective of me.

This is actually a Zoroastrian tradition. This is Los Angeles. This is the beach in Los Angeles where I used to swim, you know, daily as a teenager. These are Persian-Americans, Iranian-Americans, and they jump over fires on their New Year to cast off the bad luck of the previous year, you know, for good luck in the next year.

UNIT 4 VIDEO

The Story of Hiram Bingham

When I was eighteen, I was heading off to college, and for my birthday, my eighteenth birthday, my dad gave me a T-shirt. And on the front of the T-shirt was this, Machu Picchu, the site we're here to talk about and celebrate tonight.

This is an image from 1911. And I had heard of Machu Picchu before, but I didn't recognize the guy on the back. This was a T-shirt my dad had picked up at the Peabody Museum of Yale, which is where Bingham eventually stored a lot of his artifacts. And this was Hiram Bingham. I'd never seen his image before, but he's striking. I mean, he's very tall; he's six foot four. He's handsome. He wears jodhpurs like the best of them.

And so I got into college, I eventually came to understand why it was very exciting to go to Yale University where Bingham himself studied and where he did a lot of his work later on. But I regret to say that I did not end up becoming an archaeologist. I had, as many people do their freshman or sophomore year, a crisis, of sorts and started doing literature and history instead. But it brought me back to Latin America. And my senior year, as I was getting ready to write a senior essay, my advisor said to me, "Well why don't you write on Yale's Indiana Jones?" And, he had me at that.

Hiram Bingham, in a word, was a whirlwind. He was a force of nature. He was smart. He was deeply ambitious. He was a good organizer. He wasn't very good at staying in one place. He went to Phillips Academy in Andover and then on to Yale, where he was able to make a life for himself. He realized that he was very good at teaching his fellow students. He was extremely poor. They were extremely wealthy. He liked to read books. They liked to get notes from people who liked to read books. And he realized that he could be a teacher. However, it was very hard for him to do so because there still was a barrier of both wealth and prestige at Yale that he couldn't quite break through. Much like many of us fear and have in my case moved back to our parents' house after college, he moved back to Honolulu to be with his parents.

However, he had also by then started to think about someone who would change his life and allow him to do many things that he wanted. He'd fallen in love with Alfreda Mitchel. And Alfreda was a kind, warm, and generous person, that Bingham had met in his senior year of college. And with Alfreda they got married soon after. They would have seven sons. They came to live in very large houses in Cambridge where Bingham went to the University of Harvard, Harvard University for his doctorate, and then in New Haven.

Now, his decision to study history at Harvard was actually a fairly radical one for at the time, because he wasn't doing European history, he wasn't doing U.S. history. He was doing Latin American history, and he believed that he was the first person to ever be hired specifically to teach Latin American history in the U.S. Bingham believed that the U.S. had a future in the region that would need experts like himself in politics and economics and history to lead. After a few years

of teaching, he found himself getting anxious at being chained to teaching undergraduates, and he instead decided to embark on a new phase of his life and career as an explorer.

UNIT 5 VIDEO

Demon Fish

They can strike out of the darkness without warning. There's something about that that has us hardwired to be terrified. You would never know if a shark is coming. That, I think, both makes them scary and allows people to exaggerate the threat associated with them. Having this perception that sharks are targeting us, of course, makes it much more acceptable to target them.

I'm thrilled to talk to you about this book and I thought to begin I wanted to explain a little about how I decided to really explore this territory to begin with. You know, I've actually, I've spent the vast majority of my reporting career here in Washington covering politicians. Many people said it was obviously a natural transition from politicians to sharks.

So you saw the first recorded shark attack in history in the late 1500s comes from a Portuguese sailor who had the misfortune to fall overboard and couldn't be saved by his companions. And then if you go, you know, if you look forward there are just many tales of sharks circling around different ships and, you know, sailors, either you know basically almost kind of like a wage dispute and like a labor dispute that they complained that the captains couldn't care less if they ended up in the water with sharks and things like that and, you know, time and time again they were seen as this threat.

But sharks were still seen as a fairly abstract threat, and what changed in actually the United States and also a few other countries were when beach goers started interacting with sharks. And so, for example, this is the front page from *The Philadelphia Inquirer* referring to a series of shark strikes off the New Jersey shore in 1916. This in some ways was the inspiration for the movie *Jaws*. Again, people had been familiar with sharks, but they did not know to, you know, to what extent it could be, you know, potentially something that would come up when they went to the beach.

And so when you had four people who were killed within a span of twelve days, that was the moment when you really saw people think of sharks as, you know, a threat at any point. You know, saying "Government to aid fight to stamp out the shark horror," is that, in fact, Woodrow Wilson, who was president at the time and started his political career in New Jersey, actually came under attack for the fact that he did nothing to halt these shark strikes. And that's one thing that you see time and time again: that people somehow think that this is something that you could hold politicians accountable for.

There are actually a couple of academics, including one at Princeton, who recently found that he in fact suffered a political penalty in New Jersey, and particularly the three counties that were most affected by the drop in tourism. And so it was just interesting to see how voters really did punish Woodrow Wilson and thought that, you know, there was something he could do to ensure that they could be safe at sea.

Sources

8: "Crowding our Planet," by Thomas Hayden, NationalGeographic.com, **18:** "Climate Change Creating Millions of 'Eco Refugees,' UN Warns," by Stefan Lovgren, National Geographic News, November 18, 2005, **28:** "Boomtowns: China's Instant Cities," by Peter Hessler, *National Geographic*, June 2007, **40:** "Machisma: Brazil's Girl Power," by Cynthia Gorney, *National Geographic*, September 2011, **50:** "The Geography of Religion," by Shelley Sperry, NationalGeographic.com, **58:** *African Ceremonies*, Vol. 1, Vol. 2, by Carol Beckwith and Angela Fisher, **70:** "Marseille's Melting Pot," by Christopher Dickey, *National Geographic*, March 2012, **78:** "The Singapore Solution," by Mark Jacobson, *National Geographic*, January 2010, **86:** "Green China: Can China Go Green?" by Bill McKibben, *National Geographic*, June 2011, **99:** "China's Middle Class: Gilded Age, Gilded Cage," by Leslie T. Chang, *National Geographic*, May 2008, **107:** "U21 Ranking of National Higher Education Systems," Universitas 21, University of Melbourne, May 2012, **130:** "Bhutan's Enlightened Experiment," by Brook Larmer, *National Geographic*, March 2008, **139:** "The World According to Rome," by T. R. Reid, *National Geographic*, August 1997.

Images

Inside front cover: Robb Kendrick/National Geographic Stock, Monika Klum/National Geographic Stock, Christopher Heaney, Michael Lionstar, **1:** Aaron Mccoy/Photolibrary Collection/Getty Images, **2-3:** Ira Block/National Geographic Stock, **8:** Julio Lopez Saguar/Photographer's Choice Library/Getty Images, **9:** Steve Raymer/National Geographic Stock, **10:** FPG/Archive Photos/Getty Images, **18:** Jonathan Irish/National Geographic Stock, **19:** Jim Simmen/Photographer's Choice/Getty Images, **20-21:** Lynn Johnson/National Geographic Stock, **29:** TAO Images/Getty Images, **30-31:** Chris Johns/National Geographic Stock, **31:** Paul Chesley/National Geographic Stock, **33:** Charles D'Emery/National Geographic Stock, **34-35:** Rich Reid/National Geographic Stock, **41:** Michael Poehlman/Photographer's Choice/Getty Images, **42-43:** Pete Mcbride/National Geographic Stock, **50:** Thomas J. Abercrombie/National Geographic Stock, **52-53:** Melissa Farlow/National Geographic Stock, **58:** Abdelhak Senna/AFP/Getty Images, **59:** Frances Linzee Gordon/Lonely Planet Images/Getty Images, **59:** Martin Harvey/Peter Arnold Collection/Getty Images, **60-61:** Mattias Klum, **61:** Joel Sartore/National Geographic Stock, **63:** NASA's Earth Observatory/NOAA/DOD, **64-65:** Wu Kaixiang/Xinhua/Photoshot/Newscom, **71:** Franco Origlia/Contributor/Getty Images, **72-73:** TEK IMAGE/Science Photo Library/TEK IMAGE, **78:** David Mclain/National Geographic Stock, **79:** Scott S. Warren/National Geographic Stock, **80-81:** China Photos/Stringer/Getty Images, **86:** Greg Girard/National Geographic Stock, **87:** Greg Girard/National Geographic Stock, **88-89:** Spencer Platt/Getty Images, **89:** Bill Pugliano/Stringer/Getty Images, **91:** Grant Faint/Photographer's Choice/Getty Images, **92-93:** Joel Sartore/National Geographic Stock, **99:** Randy Olson/National Geographic Stock, **100:** Justin Guariglia/National Geographic Stock, **101:** kristian sekulic/Vetta/Getty Images, **109:** Jade/Blend Images Collection/Getty Images, **117:** Annie Griffiths/National Geographic Stock, **118-119:** Mike Theiss/National Geographic Stock, **119:** Apic/Hulton Archive/Getty Images, **121:** Hisham Ibrahim/Photographer's Choice/Getty Images, **122:** Randy Olson/National Geographic Stock, **130:** Pete Ryan/National Geographic Stock, **131:** Paul Chesley/National Geographic Stock, **132-133:** National Geographic/Getty Images, **139:** De Agostini/Getty Images, **140:** Taylor S. Kennedy/National Geographic Stock, **141:** Steve Hamblin/Alamy, **148:** Getty Images, **150-151:** Gerard Soury/Oxford Scientific/Getty Images, **151:** Topical Press Agency/Stringer/Getty Images

Nothing can stop me.....
I'm All the way UP ↑